Contents

Getting IT Right

Welcome to Getting IT Right Skills Book 3! This book will help you to extend your expertise in using a wide range of information and communication technologies.

On Target

Before you use Skills Book 3 you will already need to have a good working knowledge of a variety of the software applications covered in Skills Books 1 and 2.

You should feel yourself to be capable and confident in ICT, able to use the Windows interface without assistance, and to save your work without being reminded and to keep print-outs in your ICT folder.

In Book 3 you will learn some new packages, and also extend the skills you have in those you are already familiar with.

In the last unit you will tackle a project that involves using a mixture of software applications to solve a problem.

Skills Book 3

If you have used Skills Books 1 and 2 you will find that you are already familiar with the way that the pages are laid out. In Books 1 and 2 the names and order of the units were the same. In Book 3, however, there are some differences: the revised unit structure is explained on pages 4 and 5.

The units in Book 3 show more of the sorts of things each type of package is capable of, and the best way to approach using them. To illustrate the appropriate use and potential of the software, case-studies describe how pupils use various packages to set about solving problems.

You will need to spend time experimenting with each package. Using your previous knowledge and skills, you should not find it too difficult to work out for yourself how to use the different tools each package has – this reflects the way that many IT professionals learn.

You will find it helpful to have the appropriate software manual available for the specific application you have in your school or on a computer at home – alternatively you can use the **Help** files provided with the package.

The **IT at work** sections have been expanded to provide further insights into how ICT applications are used in a variety of industrial and commercial contexts, and the nature of the work of IT professionals.

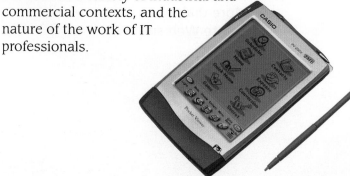

About the units

Each unit starts with its own introduction. This helps explain the sorts of everyday problems and situations in which you are likely to find ICT helpful. It also makes clear what the targets for the unit are – what you should know about and be able to do by the time you have worked through the unit.

Check that you have already covered the basic skills indicated in the **On Target** section. If you have not, you may need to go back to Book 2 to do some revision.

In the **Getting IT Right in...** section you will find some suggestions on how you might use the software in your other subjects.

At the end of each unit is a case study, called **IT at work**. These help give you an insight into how ICT is used in real-life situations.

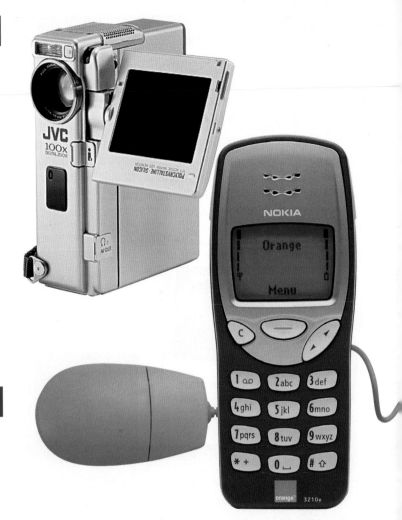

What you have to do

Work through the numbered pages in each unit in order. In some lessons you might get through several pages quite quickly, especially if you've used a similar package before.

Each double-page spread is self-contained. Read it through first, or listen carefully as your teacher takes you through it. The next step is to experiment with the various tools and actions needed to make the program work. It takes a while to get used to some of these! See if you can follow the work of the pupils to create your own versions of their files. Your teacher may be able to provide you with some ready-made data files to get you going more quickly.

On every right-hand page you'll find a very important section in the bottom corner called **What you have to do**. Your teacher will tell you which activities to do – some might be done after the lesson, and others are for those who are speeding ahead.

Always remember to save the work you do on the computer. You should also print out your work as often as possible. Keep it in a special ICT folder.

At the end of each unit your teacher will probably give you a special project to undertake. You'll be given a problem to solve, and be expected to use the computer to help you. To begin with you'll need to plan out what you need to do and when. At the end you'll need to evaluate your work.

This project will help you and your teacher to work out how well you are doing. It will show your strengths and weaknesses, and provide you with some useful targets for improvement in the next unit you do.

You can apply what you learn in this book in all your school subjects. Don't wait for your teachers to tell you to use the technology. Can you see a way in which using a computer or some other device would help you get the job done better? Don't hesitate to ask if you can do it that way!

Good luck with your work – we hope you manage to **Get IT Right!**

WHAT YOU HAVE TO DO

Unit 1 Publishing on the Web

In the first unit you will be introduced to a new type of package that will enable you to create a series of linked web pages. These are known as **web authoring** or **web editing programs**.

To begin with you will need to learn the basics. To do this you create a number of linked pages illustrating a poem. In the final section you bring these to life by adding some interactive features – text and graphics that change when you place the mouse pointer on top of them.

Unit 2 Electronic Imaging

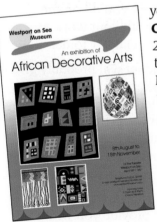

This unit will extend the work you have already done in **Graphics** in Skills Books 1 and 2. The first part looks at the tools of a more sophisticated **Draw** program, focusing on things like:

- using guides and rulers to set up grids
- working with layers
- creating complex curves
- applying a wide range of special effects.

You will create a colourful logo, letter-heading and poster for a local museum.

The second part of the unit explains how to scan images into a computer and change them using a **photo-manipulation** program. The **IT at work** case study follows how such a program was used to create an advertisement for Polaroid cameras.

Unit 3 Desktop Publishing

This unit is about **DTP** (Desktop Publishing). It shows how two pupils create a Factsheet for the museum featured in Unit 2. You can follow how a template that the museum would be able to use again was created, and then how the text and images were combined to create the final product.

Unit 4 Data Collection

This unit is about how to create a program that will sense physical data and log the results. You will need to consider different ways of presenting the information you collect, and ways in which such data can be shared.

The concluding **IT at work** case study looks at the way that the Meteorological Office uses a wide range of ICT hardware and software to prepare the weather forecast.

A remote weather station is a good example of an automatic data collection system

Unit 5 Control Systems

This unit examines how computers can be used to control events in the environment. You are introduced to the tools that you need to use to design an electronic control system.

You are then taken through the stages of building a simple system. At the end of the unit you are asked to design and build a complex system of your own.

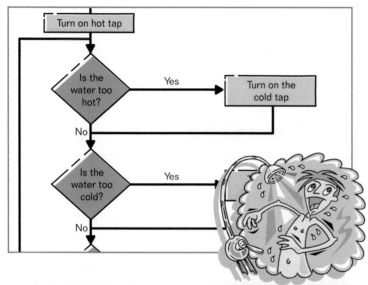

Unit 6 Spreadsheets and Databases

By now you should be familiar with using **spreadsheets** and **databases**. This unit will extend your working knowledge of them by getting you to work through the process of setting up a computer system for a video-rental shop. You will learn how to use things like **input masks** and **mail merges**.

Microsoft Excel - Video shop 1					
File Edit View Insert Format Tools Data Window Help					
	A	B	C	D	E
1	**The Video Shop**				
2					
3		APR	MAY	JUN	JUL	A
4	Rent	£250.00	£250.00	£250.00	£250.00	£2
5	Wages	£400.00	£450.00	£400.00	£425.00	£4
6	Purchases	£1,000.00	£1,200.00	£1,300.00	£1,250.00	£1,
7	Costs	£1,650.00	£1,900.00	£1,950.00	£1,925.00	£1,7
8					
9	Rentals Collected	£1,701.00	£1,862.00	£1,841.00	£1,818.00	£1,

Unit 7 Bringing IT Together

First Thoughts
Investigation
Planning
Working at the computer
Evaluation
Presentation

The final unit starts with a guide for working through your own projects. This is followed by a case study describing how a group of pupils used a range of programs to create an on-line survey into people's favourite films.

There are then a number of projects for you to tackle. Each one involves using more than one software package. You might be given a choice of projects, or be told which one to do by your teacher.

On stage

How can you use ICT to help put on the school play?

Sports day

How well run is your school's sports day? Could it be improved with a greater use of ICT?

Spring time

Can you advise a water-bottling company how to improve their quality control systems?

What's on?

A local library wants to set up an electronic *What's on?* in their area. Can you design one for them?

1 Publishing on the Web

In this unit you will learn how to create web pages that can be published on the Internet and be viewed all over the world.

On Target

You should already know how to use a **web browser** to connect to the Internet and look at web pages from all over the world. You will also need to be familiar with using a word processor, and a basic graphics package.

In this unit you will learn how to:

- create your own web pages
- use the special features that are found in a web page to make your web site active and exciting
- design your web pages for maximum impact
- organise your web pages into a web site.

On this page you will look at what a web page is, and what makes it good.

What is a web page?

A web page contains information, mainly in the form of words and pictures. It is set out rather like an ordinary document or a screen from a presentation.

A web page is designed to be looked at on the screen of your computer. You can print it out – but that is not its main purpose.

Every web page that is held on an Internet server has its own **URL** (Uniform Resource Locator), or web address. When anyone, anywhere in the world, enters that URL into their web browser, the web page will be copied onto their own computer so that they can look at it.

So the point of a web page is to be looked at. If it is easy to read and understand, and it gets across the message that you want to give, then it is a good web page.

When you make a web page remember to think about:

- what information you want to communicate
- what impression you want to make
- who your audience is.

These illustrations were taken from a school's web site. It is the site of St Louise's School in Belfast. **http://atschool.eduweb.co.uk/stlouise/index.html**

You might like to connect to this site yourself. See if you can find out the URL of any other school sites, and see what kind of thing they have done.

What is a web site?

A web site is a collection of web pages held on the same web server. For example, your school might have a web site with thousands of pages. You might want to make one of the pages on the web site. Your page will be linked to the other pages on the site.

- To find out more about what a web server is, read the panel on the right.
- To find out more about links between web pages read the section on the next page.

Learn by looking

You want your web pages to be as good as possible. Learn how to design interesting web pages by looking at lots of examples, and learning from them. When you are browsing the Internet, study the web pages you look at.

For each page think about these questions:

- Can I read it easily?
- Does it give a good impression?
- Does it have a good use of colour?
- Does it have suitable illustrations?
- Does it have a good layout?
- What would make it even better?

Learn to recognise what makes a good web page, and what features to avoid. A simple, easy-to-read page is usually more inviting than one that is cluttered with features. Large, clear text in bold colours is usually better than fiddly, pale writing.

On the Intranet

It's quite likely that your school will have an **Intranet**. An Intranet is like the Internet. The pages on the Intranet work just like Internet pages, and they are made in just the same way. However, access to an Intranet is limited to one organisation, such as a school.

If there is an Intranet at your school you can look at it without using a phone link. People outside your school cannot usually see the Intranet pages. An Intranet is a good way of sharing information between all the people in one organisation.

What is a web server?

Web pages are available to anyone over the Internet. Anyone who wants to look at a web page can download it to their computer using an Internet connection. For this to be able to happen the web page must be stored on a computer that is joined up permanently to the Internet, unlike a typical home or school computer.

A **web server** is a computer that stores web pages, and maintains a permanent link to the Internet for anyone to access. A large company, college or university might have a web server, but very few schools do. It would be too expensive.

Instead, your school might have an arrangement with an **Internet Service Provider** (ISP), or perhaps with a big college in your area. This organisation will 'host' your school's web site. That means they put all the web pages onto their web server, so that the pages can be seen by Internet users.

The home page of 'Demon', an Internet Service Provider (ISP). You will find their website at www.demon.net

WHAT YOU HAVE TO DO

1. Browse the Internet. Look at your favourite sites, or find new sites on a topic that interests you.

   Make notes as you look at the sites, about the good and bad features that you find. Think about colour, pictures, layout, and text.

2. When you have finished, write up your notes.

   - What makes a good web site?

   - What features can spoil a web site?

   Try to think of at least three examples for each question.

Links

Links between web pages add a new dimension to your work.

Web pages differ from ordinary documents and presentations in one very important way. They include links. A link is a piece of text on an area of the screen. When you click on a link a new web page is loaded into your browser.

Using this seemingly simple extra technique adds a whole new dimension to your work. On this page you will see how you can use links to improve your work.

Here is one page that a pupil made. It contains lots of links.

A link to another Internet web site

Text links to other pages on the same web site

My Links Page by Stephanie Gill

I love Boyzone: click here to go to the official Boyzone fan club page

Or see the web pages of my best friends

Nadine

Sunita

Barry

Back to my main page

Back to my school Home Page

This button is a link

The home page is the main page for the school

You will learn how to add links to your web pages on page 18.

E-commerce

In this unit you will be creating a series of linked pages that might be put on your school site, or possibly your own home page.

Many businesses and organisations design their own web sites to tell you about themselves, provide consumer information and enable you to purchase goods and services. These are known as **E-commerce** sites.

A web of links

In a book the pages are in a fixed order. This book that you are reading now is like that.

But a web site is different. The web pages are joined up by a network of links. You can look at them in any order, and jump around from page to page very easily.

For example, a teacher might make a class page, with links to one page made by each pupil in the class. From the class page you can look at any pupil's page.

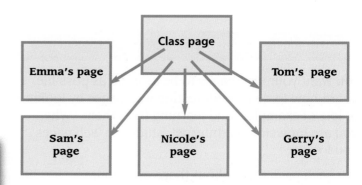

Each pupil's page will have a link back to the main class page.

There could be plenty of other links too:

● Pupils might include links to each others' pages.
● There might be links to other school pages.
● There might be links to pages elsewhere on the Internet.

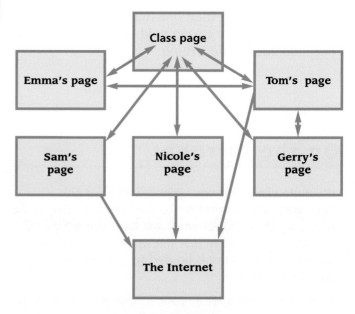

It does look a bit like a web doesn't it?

Create links *p18* Tricks with links *p20*

Short and sweet

It's not a good idea to put too much onto one web page. If you have lots of different things to say then make lots of different pages. Link them all together. People can read the pages in any order.

This means that each page will be easy to read, and will not be too cluttered.

Home page

Sometimes it can get confusing looking through a web site with lots of pages. For this reason most sites have a **home page**. This is the 'central' page of the site. From here you can get to any other part of the site.

Your school might have a home page. Your teacher might make a class home page with links to every pupil's page.

You can use this idea in your own site too. If you have lots of pages, make a central one, which links everything together.

Remember – put a link to the home page on every page you make. Then the reader can get back to the centre of the site from wherever they are in the 'web' of links.

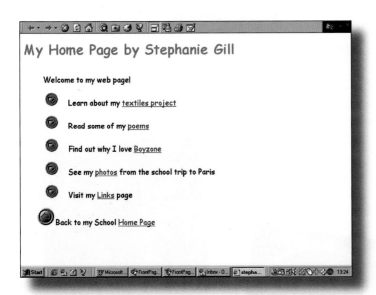

This is Stephanie Gill's home page

Getting IT Right in...

History
A class compiled records of interviews with local residents about their memories of World War 2. The interviews were added to the local museum's web site.

Art and Design
Each pupil added an electronic scan of a painting they had done during the year to a class 'Gallery' web site. With each painting there was a description of which artist it had been inspired by, and a link to a web site where further information about the artist could be found.

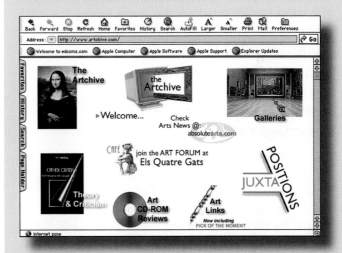

The URL of this site is www.artchive.com

WHAT YOU HAVE TO DO

1. **If your school has an Internet site, look at the home page. What headings or sections does it have?**

2. **On page 10 there is a simple map of a class home page, with links to five pupils' pages. Draw a simple map like this to show the main structure of your school web site. Don't worry about links to other sites, or links between pages, just show the main structure.**

   If you don't have a school web site, then draw a map of Stephanie Gill's site. Use her home page as a guideline.

I. Hold the FrontPage

On this page you will see how two pupils used software to create a web page that combines words and pictures.

Enter and format text

Here you will see how words and images are combined to make a web page. You can follow the example by creating the same pages yourself, or make your own web site on your own topic of interest, using the same skills.

First you will see how to enter and format the text.

FrontPage Editor

The software package used as an example in this unit is called **FrontPage Editor** (version 3.0). Other versions, or other editors, might be slightly different. However, you will still be able to follow the examples given here.

fpeditor

The project

The pupils in a class were studying famous poets for their English course. They worked in pairs. Each pair was given the name of a poet. They had to find words and pictures to make a web page about that poet to contribute to an anthology of poems which would be kept on the school's Intranet.

Lucy and Ben were assigned William Blake. To the right are two web pages they made. The two pages are 'linked'.

Adding words to the page

The **FrontPage Editor** window looks quite like a word processing package and it works in much the same way.

First, Lucy and Ben entered the text for the web page. Then they selected it and picked a suitable font.

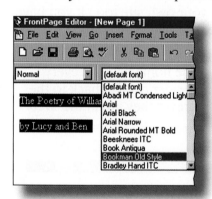

When designing web pages it's important to use only standard fonts that will be available on most people's computers. However, if the pages are going to be viewed only on computers on your school network, you should be able to use any font.

The Tyger

Tyger Tyger, burning bright,
In the forests of the night;
What immortal hand or eye,
Could frame thy fearful symmetry?

In what distant deeps or skies,
Burnt the fire of thine eyes?
On what wings dare he aspire?
What the hand, dare seize the fire?

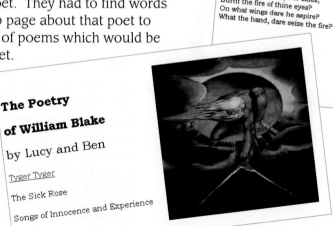

The Poetry of William Blake
by Lucy and Ben
Tyger Tyger
The Sick Rose
Songs of Innocence and Experience

Text layout using tables p16   Create a web page using a DTP package p72

Formatting text

FrontPage Editor does not let you set the font size exactly, but it lets you make the print size smaller or larger.

As you click on the large or small 'A' you will see the text grow or shrink

You can also pick text colours from this tool bar.

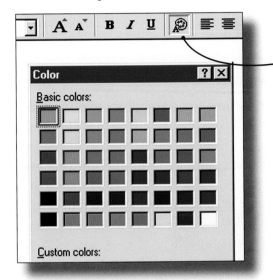

Click here to see the colour palette

FrontPage tool bar

Lucy and Ben examined the **FrontPage Editor** tool bars.

They found the icons that allowed them to:

- make text bold
- centre text
- create a bulleted list.

New line

When you are using a word processor it is easy to start a new line. You simply press **Enter** and a new line begins. If you want to leave an empty line space between two lines then press **Enter** twice.

In **FrontPage Editor** it's different. Lucy and Ben discovered that pressing **Enter** started a new line and left an empty space between lines. This meant their text was too spread out on the page.

To start a new line without leaving a big space, they held down the **Shift** key while they pressed **Enter** .

HTML

Web pages are written in a language called **HTML (HyperText Markup Language)**. Hypertext means text with links in it.

As well as the words you type into your web page, it contains hidden HTML code words. You can't normally see these code words, but they make the web page work properly. As you create your web page, **FrontPage Editor** works out the HTML you need, and writes it for you.

If you ever want to see the hidden HTML code for a web page that you have made, click on the HTML tab at the bottom of the screen. It might look something like this:

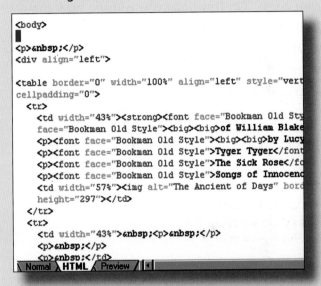

Aren't you glad that a package like **FrontPage Editor** is available to work out all the HTML for you?

Some web programmers are highly skilled in writing HTML. It gives them detailed control over what the screen will look like. They don't need to use an editor to prepare it for them.

WHAT YOU HAVE TO DO

1. Pick one of the two web pages shown on page 12, or think of the text you want to enter to create a web page of your own choice.

2. Enter and format the text.

Remember to save your work in the normal way using a suitable file name.

 13

2. Picture this

After Lucy and Ben had set up the format of the text, the next stage was to complete the web page by adding a graphic.

Adding graphics

Lucy and Ben have created a simple text-based web page. On this page you will see how they completed the task, by:

- adding a suitable illustration
- adjusting the layout
- checking the appearance of the finished work.

File formats

When your web page is posted on the Internet, anyone who wants to view it will need to **download** it, usually via a phone line and modem, onto their computer. Some items, such as bitmap graphics, have very large file sizes. These take a long time to send through a modem. For this reason you should never put bitmap graphic files into your web pages. Remember that you can recognise bitmap files because the file name ends with .BMP.

Two graphic file formats are very popular for the Internet, because they store pictures in small files that are quick to download. These are GIF files and JPG (pronounced 'jay-peg').

- GIF files usually store simple images with a small number of colours.
- JPG files usually store complex images with many colour shades (such as photographs).

Look for files in these formats. You can also convert graphics to these formats – find out more about this on page 21.

Finding a picture

Lucy and Ben knew how to add graphics to documents and presentations. Three main sources of graphics include:

- using clip art that comes free with the software you are using
- locating suitable graphics from CDs and the Internet (remember to think about copyright)
- creating your own graphics.

Lucy found a painting done by William Blake on a CD in the school library. They decided to use it.

Your graphics have to be in a suitable file format (see the panel on the left for more information about this). But don't worry – the clip art that comes with **FrontPage Editor**, and the graphics you might find on CDs and the Internet, are generally in a suitable format already.

Inserting the picture

Lucy and Ben opened the **Insert** menu and picked **Image** or **Clipart**.

The dialogue box let them choose a suitable file.

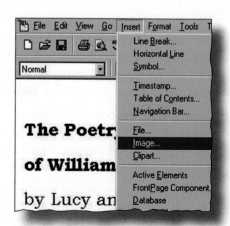

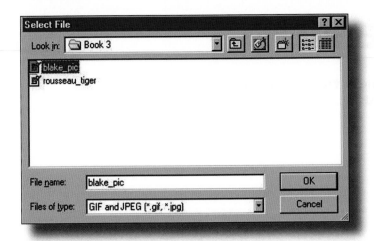

The computer looks for GIF and JPG file formats

Ben selected the file and clicked on OK.

You can also use 'cut and paste' if you are sure the graphic is in a suitable format.

Moving and resizing

This is what the page looked like with the graphic inserted:

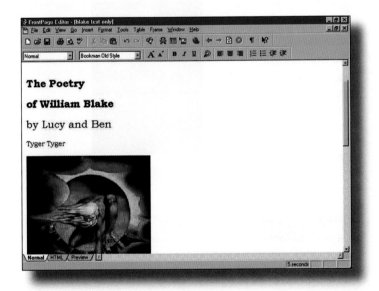

In FrontPage you can move and resize a picture, like any graphic inserted into a document. However, in many web editors you cannot adjust the wrapping of the text around the picture. Text will stay above and below the picture.

You will see how to improve the layout of the web page on pages 22–23.

Checking the page

Lucy and Ben made a quick check on the appearance of their web page. Look at the bottom of the screen, and you will see a series of tabs.

They clicked on the **Preview** tab.

The **Preview** screen gave them a quick impression of what their finished web site would look like. Use this tab any time you like, to check how your work is coming on.

Copyright

Copying pictures to use in your own private school work is usually allowed by copyright. But you have to be much more careful about the pictures you include in a public Internet site.

If you want to use a picture you find on the Internet in your own web page, why not send an e-mail to ask permission? You normally find an e-mail address on most web sites.

WHAT YOU HAVE TO DO

1. **Find a suitable illustration, and add it to your web page.**

2. **Move and resize the graphic (if you use the Blake picture, you will need to reduce it greatly in size).**

3. **Check the appearance of the web page. Save your work.**

3. Table manners

On this page you will see how to improve the layout of your web page by using tables.

Layout

FrontPage Editor is rather like a word processing package. However, compared to a modern word-processing package it gives you fewer options for the layout of text and graphics. For example, you can't 'wrap' text around a picture.

One way around this problem is to design the web page using tables. Next you will learn how to use tables in your web site.

Inserting a table

To insert a table, Lucy and Ben found this icon on the tool bar. Lucy clicked on this icon and a group of empty white squares appeared.

She clicked and dragged the mouse pointer over these squares.

All the squares she dragged the mouse over turned blue. This showed the size of the table she was making. In this picture the table has three rows and two columns.

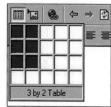

Lucy let go of the mouse button. A table of the size she chose appeared in the web page.

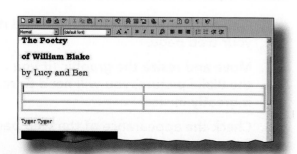

Moving text and pictures

Lucy moved the text and the picture into the table using the drag and drop technique. She could have used cut and paste instead.

Lucy used the middle row of the table, and left the rest blank for use later.

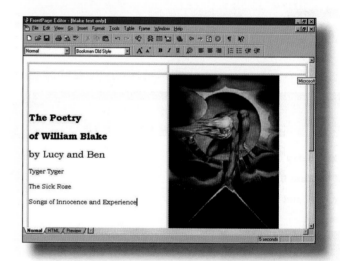

If anything goes wrong

Here are some pointers in case anything goes wrong:

- If you can't find the icon you need, open the **Table** menu, pick **Insert Table** and type in the number of rows and columns you want.

- If you pick the wrong size of table, you can add and delete rows and columns, just as you can with a table in a word processed document.

- The table will be inserted where the cursor is. Don't worry if it seems to be in the wrong place. After you drag all the text and pictures into the table, the page will completely change in appearance anyway.

Create the text *p12* Insert a picture *p14* Add special effects *p22*

The table lines can be clearly seen on the page. Ben improved the appearance of the web site by hiding them.

He right-clicked anywhere inside the table and selected **Table Properties** from the menu.

A dialogue box appeared.

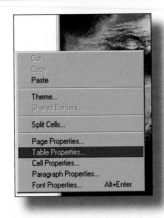

As Lucy and Ben added more features or formats to their web page, they remembered to keep checking its appearance in the web browser. This is how they did it:

After they had made a change, they clicked on the **Save** icon in the **FrontPage Editor** tool bar.

They turned to the web browser where their page was displayed, and clicked the **Refresh** icon in the tool bar.

The web browser 'loaded' the page again and they could see the effect of their changes.

Change border size to 0

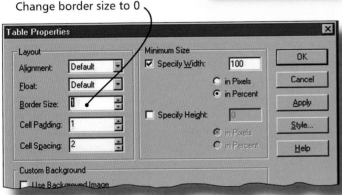

This dialogue box let him change many of the features of the table. He found the setting for **Border Size**, and changed the number from 1 to 0.

The table outline now appeared as a dotted line. It wouldn't be seen at all when the web page was downloaded.

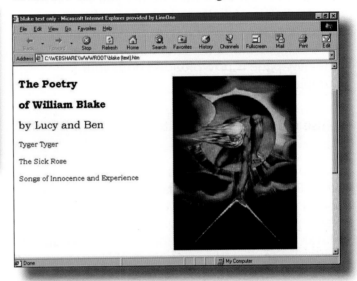

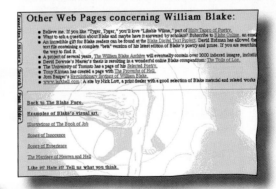

You can find out more about the poetry and pictures of William Blake by conducting an Internet search

Moving the text to the top of the cell ■

The text is aligned in the middle of the cell, half way between the top and bottom. Lucy and Ben wanted the words to start at the top of the cell, as they do in a word processed table.

Ben right-clicked in the cell where the words appear.

He picked **Cell Properties** from the menu and then found the setting for **Vertical Alignment** and changed it from **Default** to **top**.

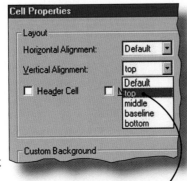

Set vertical alignment to **top**

WHAT YOU HAVE TO DO

1. **Reorganise the layout of your web page using a table.**

2. **Check what the web page looks like, displayed in a web browser.**

➡ 17

4. Link up

The next stage was for Lucy and Ben to link a number of web pages together. Clicking on links is one of the main ways to move about the Internet.

Links

If you have ever used the Internet you will know what a **link** is. A link can be a piece of text, an image, or an area of the screen. When you click on a link you are taken to another Internet page. The new page is **downloaded** onto your computer.

Links backwards and forwards

Lucy and Ben's web page lists three famous poems by William Blake. The name of each poem will be a link to a new page, showing the words of the poem and a suitable picture. The web page will also include a link backwards to the home page for the class web site.

Creating a new page

The next step was for Lucy and Ben to create the new web page, so they could link to it. The new web page would have part of the poem 'The Tyger', and a suitable picture of a tiger.

On the right is the page they created.

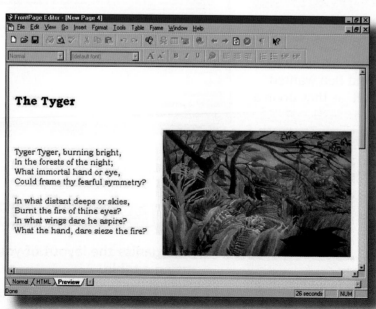

Opening both pages

Like many Windows packages, **FrontPage Editor** allows several files to be open at the same time. Ben made sure the following files were open:

- The main 'blake' page where he wanted to add the link.
- The 'Tyger, Tyger' page that he wanted to link to.

The two files could be seen on the **Windows** menu by selecting the 'blake' file.

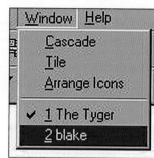

Creating the link

The 'blake' page lists the three famous poems.

In this case, the link could be the words 'Tyger, Tyger'.

Ben selected the words he wanted to turn into a link.

To create a link, he clicked on this icon on the tool bar.

Ben saw this dialogue box.

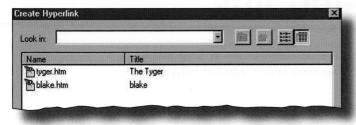

All the open files were listed at the top of the box.

He chose the 'Tyger, Tyger' file, clicked on **OK** and checked the link.

Linking to the home page

The next step was for Lucy to build in a link to the 'home page' for their class. This was not a page that she had made herself, but one that her teacher had available for her to link to on the school Intranet.

Lucy entered a link to the class home page in the top right-hand corner of their web page.

Lucy selected the top right-hand cell of the table. Then she typed the text of the home page link, (in the example here the text is right-justified).

She selected this text and clicked on the **link** icon on the tool bar. This opened the link dialogue box that she used before.

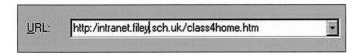

Lucy could have linked to the home page using a URL. She could have entered the **URL** in the empty space available and clicked on **OK**.

However, Lucy decided to link to the home page using a file name. She clicked on this icon.

A familiar looking dialogue box appeared. It looked like the dialogue box she used when she opened a file. Lucy used this box to locate and select the file she wanted to link to, and clicked on **OK**.

The link was now complete. She saved the web page, and checked that the link worked.

Completing the web pages

In order to complete the links required for the web site, Ben added a link back from the 'Tyger' page to the 'blake' page.

He used the techniques he had learned to add a link to the Tyger page, linking it back to the blake page.

Finally, Ben created an extra web page and linked it into the site.

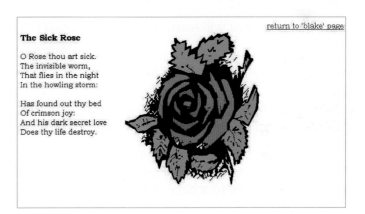

WHAT YOU HAVE TO DO

1. **Follow what Lucy and Ben did on this page, so that you have two web pages – 'Blake' and 'Tyger Tyger'.**

2. **Add links so that each page has a link to the other.**

3. **Add a link from the 'Blake' page back to your class home page.**

4. **Create the 'Sick Rose' web page and add it to the site.**

5. The missing link

There are many other ways Lucy and Ben could use links to enhance their web sites. You can learn about some of these ways on this page.

More tricks with links

You have learned to create text links to other web pages within the same web site. But there are many other interesting things that you can do with links. You can:

- link to other web sites
- use pictures as links
- help people to send e-mails to you.

On this page you will learn these 'tricks with links'.

The hyperlink icon

The URL of this site is http://blake.bellevue.com

Linking to other web sites

A web page can include links to other web sites, anywhere on the Internet. For example, Lucy and Ben could include a link to a page with more details about William Blake.

It is very easy to include such a link. Ben simply:

- searched the Internet to find a site which might be of interest to people reading their web page
- noted down the URL (or he could have copied it into the clipboard)
- created a link to that URL, using the techniques shown on the previous page.

Ben spent one lesson searching the Internet for a suitable web site. He found a site which had a lot of information about Blake, and plenty of links to other sites too.

Next, Ben created a link in the bottom right-hand corner of the page.

He entered the text he wanted to use as a link. Then he selected it and clicked the **Hyperlink** icon. Finally, he entered the URL into the link dialogue box.

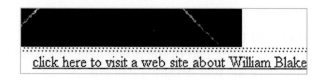

click here to visit a web site about William Blake

A picture link

Any picture, or part of a picture, can be used as a link.

Lucy decided to add another link – a picture of a 'home'. When someone clicked on this picture, they would return to the home page. The completed link looked like this.

Click here to go to our class home page

To create this link, Lucy created a suitable image, in a suitable graphic format. She inserted this image into the web page and created a graphic link from the image.

i Adding links – basics *p18* Inserting pictures *p14* Using e-mail links in a project *p132*

Creating the image

Lucy used **Paint** to create the image, because this was a package she was familiar with. It was important for the image to be very small, with the minimum white space around it. In most packages, it is possible to reduce the available space to a very small square. In Paint, the white area of the screen represents the size of the image.

Lucy clicked and dragged the lower right-hand corner of this white area, to reduce it to a very small size. In the resulting small area of screen, she created a small picture of a house.

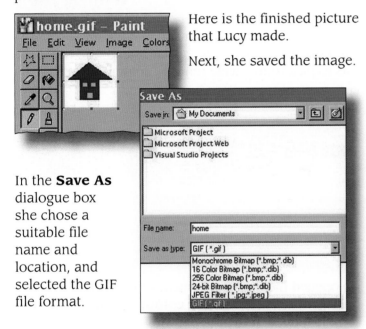

Here is the finished picture that Lucy made.

Next, she saved the image.

In the **Save As** dialogue box she chose a suitable file name and location, and selected the GIF file format.

Now the graphic was suitable for use on a web site.

Creating the link

To insert the graphic into the web page Ben clicked on the inserted image to select it and clicked on the **Hyperlink** icon. Then he created a link to his class home page.

Now, when anyone clicked on the picture of the house at the top of the screen, they would link to his class home page.

An e-mail link

Many web sites include an **e-mail link**. If someone clicks on such a link their e-mail program starts up, and creates an e-mail addressed to the person who made the site. This is a good facility to use if you want to ask permission to link to the site, or to copy an image from the site.

An e-mail link can be either a piece of text, or an image.

Ben found it easy to create an e-mail link on their web site. He entered the text and inserted the image that he wanted to use as a link. Then he selected it and clicked on the **Hyperlink** icon.

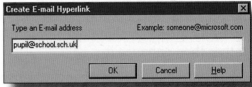

The usual dialogue box appeared, and he clicked on the 'e-mail' icon, and entered their school's e-mail address.

This is what the 'blake' web page looked like with all the links in place.

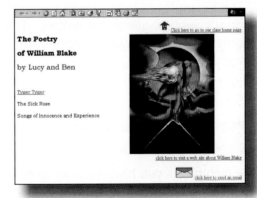

Make sure you get permission from your teacher before you enter your e-mail address into a public web site.

WHAT YOU HAVE TO DO

1. **Look for e-mail links, and picture links in the sites you visit on the Internet.**

2. **Add at least one example of a picture link and an e-mail link to your own web pages.**

6. www.hatever next?

On this page learn about some additional ways that you can use graphics and colour to spice up your web site.

More uses of graphics

There are many ways in which graphic features can be used to make a web site more attractive or more exciting.

But beware! Over-use of graphical tricks and features can spoil your web page. The screen can become too complex and cluttered. Too many fancy features can hide the content of the page, rather than enhance it.

Don't aim to include all the features shown here on one web page. Choose features carefully, just as you would be careful about the use of different fonts and layouts in a text document.

The examples here are taken from different pupils' web pages about writers. They picked only one special graphic feature for each web page.

Background colour ■

The web pages you have seen up to now have used the following colours:

- the background is **white**
- the text is **black**
- the links are **blue**
- the links change to **purple** after they have been used.

These are the **default** web page colours.

Colin made a site about the writer Ernest Hemingway. He used colour creatively to enhance the site.

Setting the background colour ■

Colin opened the **Format** menu and picked **Background**. A dialogue box appeared. He could use this to pick from a wide range of colours.

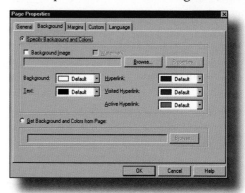

He opened the drop down menus to pick the **background colour**, **text colour**, and **link colour**.

Background image ■

The web pages you have seen up to now included an image as part of the page. But there is an alternative. You can use an image to make the background to your web page.

Harry created a page about HP Lovecraft, who wrote horror stories about a monster called

Cthulu. He found a picture of Cthulu on the Internet.

Harry used this image as the background to his web site. Because the image is smaller than the page it is repeated. The next page shows what the site looked like. Harry changed the font colour too.

Ernest Hemingway

Hemingway was a soldier, a hunter, a big-game fisherman and a man of action. He was also sometimes a lonely and sad man who drank to excess. He invented the modern style of adventure writing, with short sentences and fewer fancy words.

To find out more about his novels click here.

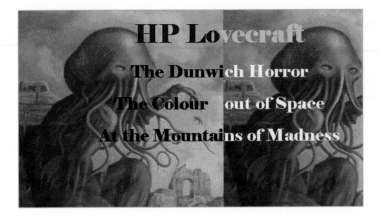

Some people might think this page looks a bit too cluttered – that's the trouble with background images. Others might like this effect because it looks quite dramatic. What do you think?

Julie created a page about the Hercule Poirot stories by Agatha Christie. She wanted her web site to look rather elegant and sophisticated. She found a picture that looked like polished granite.

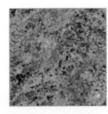

She used this as a background image. Here is what the web page looked like. (Julie chose the font carefully too.)

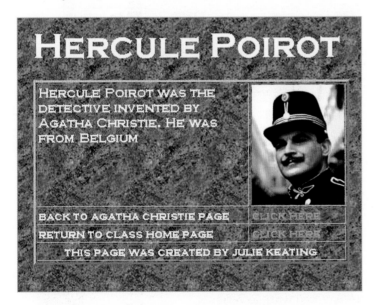

The image that is used to make the background to the site is **tiled** by the computer. This means it is repeated over and over until the whole screen is filled. On the Cthulu page you can tell that the image is repeated. On the Poirot page the tiling blends together to produce a smooth effect. It depends what type of image you choose.

A web site is not fixed in place like a book. You can add movement and change to it. This is a big subject, and if you are interested you will have to read specialist books about web page design. However, in this book you can learn several interesting features that will liven up your site.

One of these features is animated text – i.e. text that moves on the screen.

Harry decided to make the words on the Cthulu page drop down one by one from the top of the screen into place – quite a sinister effect. Here is how he did it:

First he selected all the text he wanted to animate.

Then he opened the **Format** menu and selected **Animation**.

Finally he selected the type of text animation he wanted.

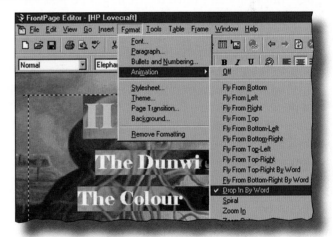

It is difficult in a book to show what this looks like on the Internet, but below is a snapshot of Harry's page, while the animation was running. Can you see the word 'out' is halfway down the page, dropping into place?

You need to be aware that some older web browsers do not display animated text, and some new ones can be set up so that animation doesn't work. You will still see the words, but they won't move.

7. Making it a hit

On the final page of this unit you will look at how to give web pages interactive features – words and pictures that the viewer can change.

A picture that changes ■

A part of a web page can also be made to change by adding a **Hover Button**.

● A hover button can display words or an image.

● A hover button can work as a link to another web page, but it doesn't have to – it might be just for display.

● The most interesting feature of a hover button is that you can set it up so that when the mouse pointer 'hovers' over the button it changes automatically to show different words or a different image.

It is hard to show how a hover button works in a book, because you really have to see it in action, but here is an example.

Leanne created a page about 'Alice in Wonderland'. She found two images that she liked.

She didn't know which one to use in her web page. So she decided to use a hover button, and display both images.

On the right is what her web page looked like normally.

Below is what it looked like if you moved the mouse pointer over the picture.

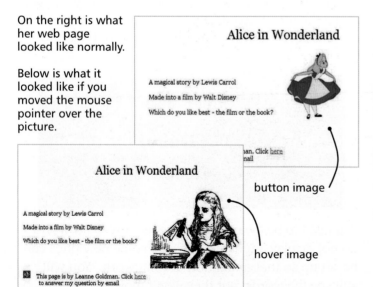

button image

hover image

How to insert a Hover Button ■

Here is how Leanne added a hover button to her web page. She opened the **Insert** menu, selected **Active Element** and then she selected **Hover Button**.

This dialogue box appeared.

button text

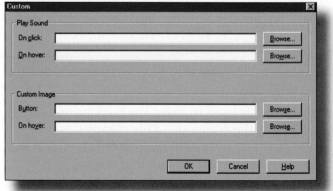

custom button

Next she deleted the **Button text**, and clicked on the **Custom** button.

A second dialogue box appeared, which looked like this:

i Other special effects *p22* Using web publishing skills *p132*

Using this dialogue box Leanne set:

- the **Button** image (what the button normally shows)
- the **Hover** image (what the button shows when the mouse pointer hovers over it.

Here is how she did it. She clicked on the **Browse** button and selected the image she wanted to use from where it was stored on her computer system.

She made sure she set the button image and the hover image. When she had set the images, she clicked on **OK**. Then she clicked on **OK** again to insert the button into her web site.

A button can be treated like any other image. It can be moved around the web site, inserted into tables, and made larger or smaller. Make sure the button is big enough to show all of your chosen image.

You won't be able to see the image changing until you 'preview' the page in a web browser.

Adding a hit counter

Once Leanne had set up her web page, and posted it to the Internet she wondered if anyone had downloaded it and looked at it.

There was an easy way to find out. She simply added a **hit counter** to her page. A hit counter counts up the number of times anyone has looked at your web page. This feature won't work with all editors and browsers, but it is worth knowing about.

Leanne added a **hit counter** to her Alice page. Here is what she did.

First she added some text to her web page, to tell people what the hit counter was. Then she selected the place where she wanted the hit counter to appear. Next she opened the **Insert** menu and picked **Active Elements** and **Hit Counter**.

A dialogue box appeared. She picked the style of counter she wanted to use and clicked on **OK**.

Below is what the counter looked like on the page.

> How many people have looked at my web page? 7

Other effects

There are many other ways to produce special effects on your web page. If you are interested you might like to investigate some of the following:

- adding sounds
- inserting **animated gifs** (moving images) into your web site
- formatting text so that it moves around the screen, or blinks on and off
- using programming features like JAVA to make your web sites interactive (for experts only).

On Target

You should now know how to:

- create your own web pages
- use the special features that are found in a web page to make your web site active and exciting
- design your web pages for maximum impact.

WHAT YOU HAVE TO DO

1. Look out for the features mentioned here, when you are browsing the web.
2. Add one of the features from this section to your web page.
3. Pick one of the other features mentioned in this section, and write instructions suitable for a pupil of your age, telling them how to add that feature to their web page.
4. Read the IT at work case study on the next page.

IT at work

Zoom.co.uk is an e-commerce site – a shopping mall on the Internet. Here you will learn how it was founded, and why it looks the way it does.

Cyberia

Zoom's managing director is Eva Pascoe. She is their online marketing director. In the mid-1990s she made her name as the co-founder of the Cyberia Group, the UK's best-known chain of cyber-cafés. Her original aim was to set up an IT training centre for women. The cafés were a way of creating a more social and relaxed environment, with coffee, cakes and croissants.

Since then Cyberia cafés have sprung up all over the world. In the late 1990s Eva sold most of her stake in the venture and joined Arcadia.

Arcadia

Arcadia is a conglomerate of high street fashion shops including Burtons, Dorothy Perkins, Hawkshead and TopShop.

Here Eva set up and runs Zoom, an Internet site where people can buy a wide range of clothes and other products. It is already one of the most successful sites on the Internet. Founded in 1999, it has already cornered 40% of the UK Internet clothes shopping market.

Eva Pascoe is often asked why it's called Zoom. The company were looking for a name that would be open to everybody and would not sound like technology. A name like 'Double Click' would have sounded rather 'tech-y'. They were looking for something that was fast, wired and ahead of the game, and 'Zoom' seemed to fit the bill. The stripes symbolise speed and give a sense of movement. They wanted to be energetic to get people to come with them.

The Zoom.co.uk web site was designed to be a refreshing change. The five basic colours used are strong and fresh. The typeface, graphics and colours communicate direction and navigation. Simple language using strong individual words indicates how to travel through the site quickly to get to the required information. Graphics are all designed for high-speed download to save the customer time.

Eva is convinced that clothes shopping by Internet will come to be as popular as walking down the high street. It is its sheer convenience that seems to be the main selling point.

Man at Zoom

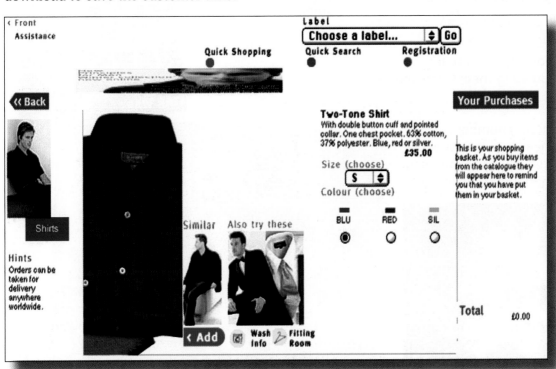

Most men hate shopping for clothes, so any man out there is a potential Zoom customer. Some men find visiting a big store very stressful. But if they shop online for clothes it only takes a few minutes, and it's done. They can now be in control of their own fashion acquisitions.

2 Electronic Imaging

Electronic imaging means creating lines, shapes, forms, colours, textures and patterns using electronic means. In this unit you will be looking at how to use a computer and other equipment to create logos and posters, and to make changes to photographs.

On Target

You should already know how to:

- use a range of basic tools in bitmap and vector paint and drawing packages
- develop a graphic design on screen that achieves the result you want
- create images that communicate a specific message to the intended audience.

In this unit you will develop these skills by:

- using a wider range of tools in a drawing package
- applying some basic principles of communication, design and layout
- learning how to import images into a computer and manipulating them using special software.

You will follow the work of a number of pupils as they design a letter-head and then a poster for a local museum. Then you will experiment with scanning in and changing some images.

Using visual images

Some things can be best communicated using words. On other occasions a picture or diagram delivers the information quickly and clearly. Often a combination of the two gets the message across.

Many forms of communication use a complex mixture of words and pictures to inform, attract attention and create an impact. Some obvious examples are posters, magazines, CD covers, book jackets, etc.

It's a digital world

Until quite recently most graphic products were created by highly skilled specialists. They used papers, pens, pencils, paints and photographs to prepare the original 'artwork' which could then be printed from.

Today, although ideas still start on paper, most of the development work is done 'on screen'. A variety of different computer programs enable the designer to experiment quickly and easily, and to achieve effects that would take a long time to do by hand. Powerful visual elements such as distortion, perspective, gradation, transparency and shadows take seconds to create. And, when the design is finished, it can be sent down a high-speed Internet connection to arrive anywhere in the world just a few moments later.

Good design

There are some simple guidelines that will help you create successful graphic images:

- **Be repetitive** – use a small number of identical or very similar elements frequently, rather than lots of different ones.

- **Use contrast** – include one element (a shape, or colour, perhaps) that is completely different from all the rest.

- **Line things up** – use horizontal and vertical guides to help visually tie different graphic elements together.

- **Include some space** – don't try to fill every part of the paper (or screen) with text or images. Some visual space is needed, just as spaces between sentences and paragraphs give the reader a chance to pause for a moment …

… and finally, most important of all,

- **Keep it simple** – avoid the temptation to include all those special effects you've just discovered. One is usually quite enough!

You will see all these guidelines being used by various pupils in this unit in the designs they develop, and in the following unit on desktop publishing.

Using the visual language

When you speak or write in English, or any other language, there are rules to be used (called grammar). Provided everyone understands the rules, they will understand the message. But the way the words are written makes a difference too – they can be made to sound threatening, or friendly, for example.

Creating visual images works in a similar way. There are certain visual styles we all understand. At the same time particular lines, shapes, forms, colours, textures and patterns can be put together to create a strong visual style that can make us react in certain ways.

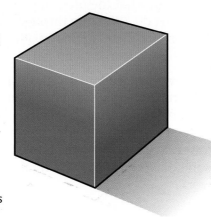

This is not a three-dimensional box – it's a two-dimensional drawing that we 'read' as being three-dimensional

There's nothing new...

Very few designs are completely original, so you don't need to make yours so. Get into the habit of noticing examples of design and the use of electronic imaging techniques in the everyday graphic products you use. Sometimes you can spot a particular effect that you know can only be created in one particular software package.

It may be that you see a CD cover with a particular textured effect, and then a chocolate box with a particular colour scheme that catches your eye, and a clever use of a style of lettering. Later, when you're trying to think of an idea for a poster, you might want to try combining a similar texture with a variation of the lettering you saw.

By the time you have finished the drawing section of this unit you should be able to identify all the tools that have been used to create this image electronically

Planning IT

As with all your ICT work, remember that planning is important. Don't just sit down at the computer and hope something good happens. Before you start, make sure you have a good idea of what you are trying to achieve. Think about:

● what words and images need to be included

● what style it needs to have

● who the audience is.

You should keep some evidence of this in your ICT folder in the form of notes and sketches.

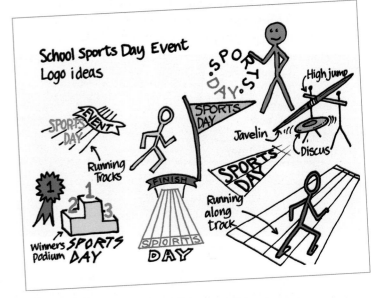

Trying IT out

Computers are excellent tools for **experimentation**. You can try things out to see what happens without fear of breaking something or destroying something you've already spent hours on (providing you've remembered to save it first, of course!). Before you get down to planning a design you will need to have found out what the program you are going to use can and can't do. Working through this unit will help you do this, but there are many other tools that there just isn't the space to explain here.

However well-planned your design is on paper, when you come to create it on the computer it sometimes just doesn't look right. Maybe a particular shape needs to be a little lighter or darker, further up or lower down, or perhaps in front of, or behind, something else. Keep trying things out until they work.

Getting IT Right in...

Art and Design

Art and Design is particularly concerned with creating visual images. You will find that bitmap programs such as **PaintShop Pro, Painter, Photo Paint** or **Photoshop** require you to think in a similar way about colour, form and light as you would if using paint or other traditional artists' materials.

(These packages are described in more detail on pages 50–57.)

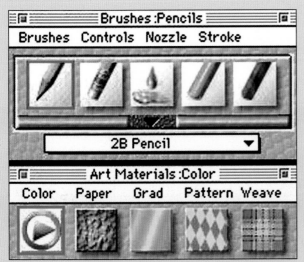

Design and Technology

Many D&T projects include the production of graphic products, such as packaging and logos. Any of the 2D vector packages such as **CorelDRAW, Serif Draw** or **Illustrator** will help make it easier and quicker for you to create high quality artwork. If you are developing designs for 3D products there are a number of graphic and **CAD/CAM** (Computer-aided Design/Computer-aided Manufacture) packages, though these tend to be complicated to use.

Media Studies

If you are asked to produce newspapers, magazines, advertisements, etc., you will certainly find many of the packages covered in this unit helpful. Special software is available that enables you to edit moving images, sound and music.

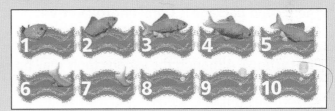

Evaluating IT

As your work progresses you need to keep asking yourself how well it's going. For example, your new idea for a colour scheme and changing one of the photographs might appeal to you, but does it help make the image suitable for the intended audience?

Discuss your work with other people, and listen to their suggestions. You may not always agree with them, but you'll often find just explaining what you are doing and difficulties you may be having helps give you some new ideas.

You will also need to evaluate the hardware and software you've chosen to use. Is it better to use an electronic scanner or a digital camera, or perhaps clip art would be better, or possibly quicker? Does the program enable you to achieve the complexity you need, or are you struggling to use a package where something simpler would have done the job just as well? Maybe even a computer wasn't the best tool to use in the first place?

If I were you I'd start again!

WHAT YOU HAVE TO DO

Start a collection of graphic products, e.g. leaflets, logos, packaging, etc. Make notes to suggest how a graphics program could have been used to create the words and images.

I. At the interface

Below is the main screen of CorelDraw. You need to become familiar with its layout and what the different roll-up windows will enable you to do.

Menus and tools

In this unit you'll be using two main packages. The first is **CorelDraw V4**, a vector drawing program. You may have a different version of this program, or maybe another similar one, such as **SerifDraw**.

The second package is **Corel PhotoPaint V4**. Again you may have a different version or a different type, such as **PaintShop Pro** or **Photoshop**. Although the various tools may be in different places on the screen, they all work in very similar ways.

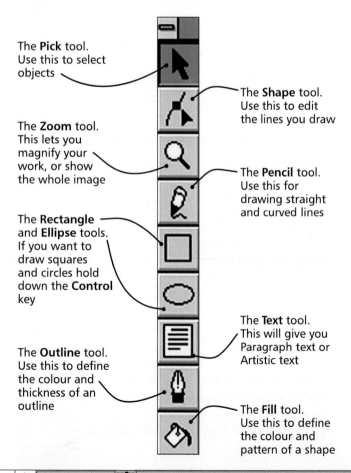

The **Pick** tool. Use this to select objects

The **Shape** tool. Use this to edit the lines you draw

The **Zoom** tool. This lets you magnify your work, or show the whole image

The **Pencil** tool. Use this for drawing straight and curved lines

The **Rectangle** and **Ellipse** tools. If you want to draw squares and circles hold down the **Control** key

The **Text** tool. This will give you Paragraph text or Artistic text

The **Outline** tool. Use this to define the colour and thickness of an outline

The **Fill** tool. Use this to define the colour and pattern of a shape

i Using the text roll-up window *p36* Keyboard shortcuts *p37* Uniform fill *p38*

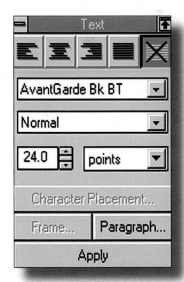

In CorelDRAW, 'drop-down' windows are called 'roll-up' windows!

The **Text roll-up window** enables you to change the typeface, weight and size of lettering quickly

You can also click to align paragraphs to the left, right or centre

G o for it!

Go for it!

Go for it!

Go for it!

If you want to see your image without all the tool bars and roll-ups, press **F9** . If you have a very complex image in a Draw program, or your computer is not very fast, you might find it quicker to move objects around using a **wireframe** view (**Shift** + **F9**).

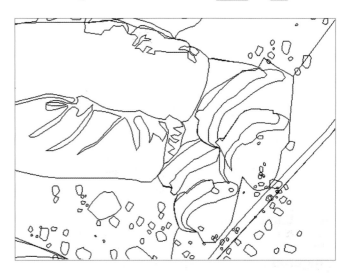

The **Fill roll-up window** is opened up from the Fill icon in the tool bar. This is the quickest way to apply a variety of fills, blends and patterns

Blend

2-colour tile fills

Full colour tile fills

Texture selection

Blend patterns

Colour selection

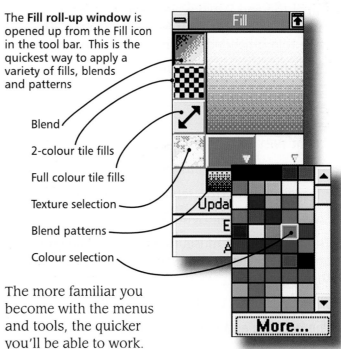

The more familiar you become with the menus and tools, the quicker you'll be able to work.

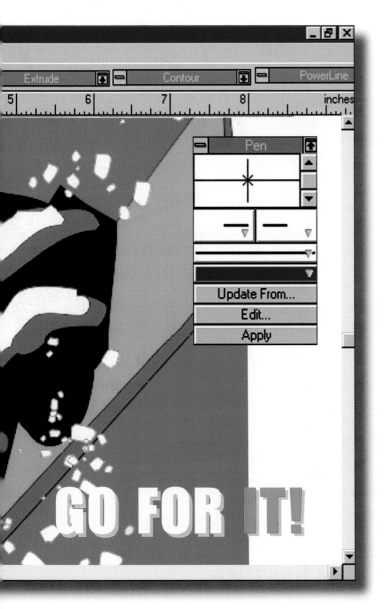

WHAT YOU HAVE TO DO

Open your Draw program. Explore and experiment with the various tools and menus. Make some notes about what you discover they can do.

2. Take a letter

On this page you will see how two pupils made a start with the design of a simple graphic logo for a letter-head.

Back to basics

There are a number of basic procedures that need to be understood and applied when using a graphic drawing package. These involve:

- setting up the page format
- setting up margins, guides and rulers.

The brief

Samantha and David were asked by a local museum to design a letter-head and logo. They were told it needed to contain the following text:

Westport on Sea Museum

18 The Parade

Westport on Sea

Kent WP1 1XU

Telephone: 01234 56789

E-mail: westportmuseum@linetwo.net

www.westportmuseum.edu

The fact that the museum was in a seaside town and small fishing port needed to be reflected in the graphics.

The paper to be used was plain white A4.

The heading and logo were to be contained in the top 50mm.

No more than two colours, plus black, could be used.

Starting point

Sam and Dave began by discussing the project. The brief was clear and concise and meant they could get straight down to designing the main logo. They started by making a list of seaside and fishing words that also conjured up some possible **images**.

Sand
Sun
Seagulls
Fishing nets
Bucket and spade
Waves
Surf

Then they talked about **colour**. A scheme based on blues (sky and sea) and yellows (sun and sand) seemed highly appropriate.

Next was **font**. A museum suggested something historical, classical and traditional, such as Times New Roman. However, the museum itself was bright and airy and didn't seem old-fashioned at all.

At the other extreme, something highly ornate, decorative or computer-age didn't seem right either. They decided to leave this until they were using the computer, and could experiment with some different fonts on screen.

Opening Draw

Sam and Dave opened their **Draw** program. It automatically opened a new file, which they immediately named and saved in their own area.

First they checked that the **Paper Size** and **Format** was correct (i.e. A4 portrait) by looking in **Page Size**. They opened this by clicking on **Page Setup** in the **Layout** menu. They needed to change the paper size to A4 portrait.

They also opened **Print Setup** in the **File** menu, ready for when they wanted to print out. They also needed to re-set the paper size here too.

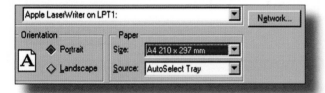

Setting margins and guides

Next they placed a number of margin guides. These appear on screen, but don't print out. They are very useful for making sure everything lines up. To create the guides they clicked on a ruler and dragged a guide out onto the paper. Sam used the measurements on the other ruler to make sure it was 'dropped' in exactly the right place.

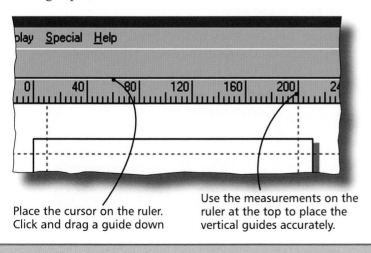

Place the cursor on the ruler. Click and drag a guide down

Use the measurements on the ruler at the top to place the vertical guides accurately.

Sam placed two vertical margin guides 15mm from each edge, and two horizontal guides 10mm and 50mm from the top. To do this accurately they used the **Zoom** tool to go in closer.

This clearly identified the space they had to work in.

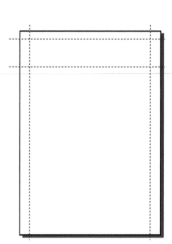

Show rulers

You may need to check that **Show Rulers** is selected in the **Display Menu**.

To change the ruler measurements to metric, open the **Grid Setup** menu from the **Layout** menu and change the **Grid Frequency** settings as shown.

Change these to millimetres

To set rulers to 0,0 at the edge of your paper, pull them from the top left corner of the box to the top left corner of your page.

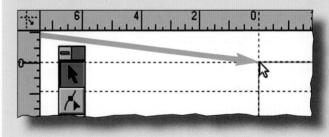

WHAT YOU HAVE TO DO

Follow Sam and Dave's actions.

- **Open your Draw package.**
- **Check the page size and orientation.**
- **Set the margin guides.**

3. Blue moods

Next you will see how Samantha and Dave started to design the logo for the museum. First they needed to choose the font and its colour.

Designing the logo

On this page you will see how to use the Text roll-up window and the Line tool. Then you will learn about setting the colour.

Using the text roll-up window ■

Sam and Dave felt that the full name of the museum needed to appear in the logo, so they began by typing this in. They clicked on the **Text** tool, and placed the cursor roughly where they wanted the text. The letters they typed in appeared in the default typeface and size.

Sam knew that they could easily alter the position of the text and its appearance later.

Dave then went to **Text** and **Text Roll-Up** to bring the **Text roll-up window** onto the screen.

Dave highlighted the text. They scrolled through some of the different fonts that had been installed on their computer, and discussed them as they appeared.

They noted down a couple of possibilities they liked. Down at the bottom of the list they came to one called VAGRounded BT. They immediately thought that this was what they were looking for – it was plain and easy to read yet modern-looking.

Click on **Apply** to check what it looks like on the page

Getting in line ■

Sam's next idea was to underline the name in a thick coloured line. First she clicked on the **Outline** tool.

She positioned the cursor where she wanted the line to start. Holding down the Control key at the same time she clicked once and dragged to the right until she got to the point where she wanted the line to end. Then she clicked again.

Next she used the **Pick** tool to select the line, and then clicked on the **Outline** tool. This opened up a sub-menu with more icons on.

Sam clicked on the thickest line

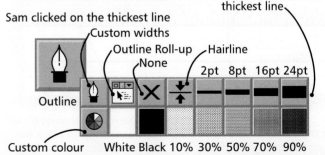

Kind of blue

Next Sam clicked on the Outline colour wheel icon (also in the Outline tool option). This opened the **Outline Color** dialogue box.

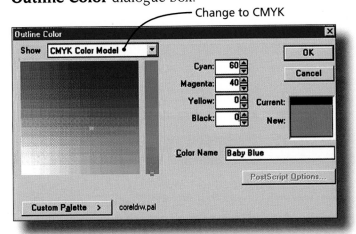

Here Sam changed the colour settings to CMYK. (See the grey panel to the right for an explanation of CMYK.) These give a very precise control of colours. She scrolled through the available colours until she got to all the blues. Dave agreed with her that 100% Blue (100% Cyan, 100% Magenta, 0% Yellow and Black) was too dark, so they tried one that was 60% Cyan, 40% Magenta, 0% Yellow and 0% Black. This one was called **Baby Blue**. When they saw it applied to the line they thought it represented the sea and sky well.

Outline and fill

In Draw packages, both shapes and letters have an **outline** and a **fill** area. The thickness of an outline can be varied, and its colour changed. The fill colour can be made to be white, black or a colour.

Calling the colours

There are two main methods of describing colours accurately, called RGB and CMYK. These initials stand for Red, Green and Blue, and Cyan, Magenta, Yellow and Black. A colour can be defined by stating either the exact percentages of each in a mixture of these colours (e.g. 10% Red, 60% Green, 70% Blue), or a reference on a scale of 255 gradations (e.g. R75, G0, B255).

If the image that is being created is to be viewed on screen, then the RGB model is used. This is because red, green and blue light are fired onto the screen. 100% Red, 100% Green and 100% Blue combine together to show white. 0% of each shows black.

If however the image is to be printed, then the CMYK model is used. This is because cyan, magenta, yellow and black inks are used to create coloured prints.

Take the shortcut

Keyboard shortcuts are combinations of keys on the keyboard you can press to immediately access tools or menus or undertake actions. Packages such as CorelDRAW have hundreds of keyboard shortcut alternatives. Below are some of the main ones you will need to use as you work through this unit.

Duplicate	Ctrl + D
Convert to curves	Ctrl + Q
Undo last action	Ctrl + Z
Group together	Ctrl + G
Ungroup	Ctrl + U
Artistic text	Ctrl + T
Print Dialogue	Ctrl + P
Send to back	Shift + Page Down
Bring to front	Shift + Page Up
Text roll-up	Ctrl + F2
Wireframe	Shift + F9
Outline Pen	F12

WHAT YOU HAVE TO DO

Follow Sam and Dave's actions.

1. **Place and style the museum name text.**

2. **Add a thick blue line underneath.**

4. Sun, sea and circles

On this page you can follow how Sam and Dave created the wave shape and sun motif.

Working with curves

Next you will see how to use circles and curves in your graphic work.

Bezier curves

Most Draw packages have a conventional line drawing tool that can be used to create freehand and 'constrained' straight lines. They also include a tool that enables **Bezier curves** to be drawn. These produce regular, flowing curved lines.

Bezier curves are fun to experiment with, but quite difficult to control until you really get the hang of them.

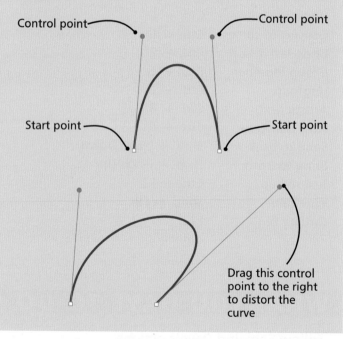

Control point — • — Control point

Start point — — Start point

Drag this control point to the right to distort the curve

Sun-spots

Sam and Dave decided to move on to creating their sun shape. They selected the **Ellipse** tool. By holding down the **Control** key at the same time as dragging the mouse across the screen they were able to draw a regular circle. They used the **Pick** tool to select the circle, and clicked on the **Fill** tool to open the **Uniform Fill** dialogue box.

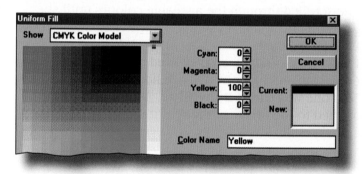

This time they set up a pure yellow to fill the circle. Using the **Pen** tool and clicking on the **Line** icon, they removed the black outline.

Next they moved the sun into the top left-hand corner of the page. The sun covered the name and blue line.

Sam highlighted the sun and went to the **Arrange** menu and the **Order** sub-menu. Here she clicked on **To Back** to place the sun behind the text and blue line.

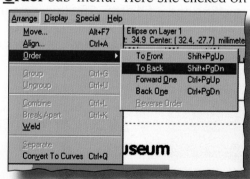

i At the interface *p32*

Now their logo looked like this:

Convert to curves

Dave wanted to do some experiments. He created a duplicate of the sun by clicking on **Control** + **D** and moved it to the middle of the screen. Then he clicked on **Control** + **Q** to Con**v**ert To **Curves**. Next he clicked on the **Shape** tool.

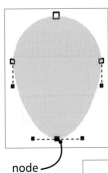

node

This enabled him to start pulling the circle out of shape.

When he pulled the bottom node up to the top right, he created a very unexpected and interesting shape.

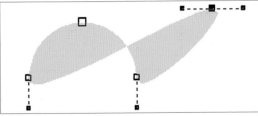

It took him a long time to pull it into just the shape he wanted – it needed to be smooth and flowing to represent a wave. He also changed the colour to **Baby Blue** and put it in place of the straight blue line.

Sam and Dave talked to Peter and Gordon, who suggested that the logo might be better balanced if the word 'Museum' was on the next line.

To see their final logo without the guide lines, Sam zoomed in on it and pressed F9 .

Adding the address

Finally, Dave added the museum's contact details that they had been given. They chose AvantGarde Bk BT as a font and made the main address 12pt. They added a line space and made the other details slightly smaller at 10pt.

They decided to align the text to the right-hand margin. To do this they selected the block of text, and clicked on the icon shown on the right. Finally, they used another ruler guide to line the top up with the top of the name of the museum on the left.

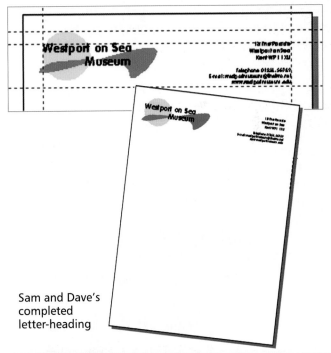

Sam and Dave's completed letter-heading

WHAT YOU HAVE TO DO

Follow Sam and Dave's actions to complete the letter-head.

1. **Create and position the sun and wave shapes.**

2. **Add the address and print out a copy.**

5. Out of Africa

Westport on Sea Museum were delighted with the letter-head Sam and Dave had designed for them. They decided to ask them if they could design a poster for a forthcoming exhibition.

Designing a poster

Sam and Dave were told that the poster should be A4 portrait size. 25 copies were to be printed out on a full-colour inkjet printer (or colour photocopied from an original) and put up around the town. The exhibition was a collection of decorative arts (i.e. textiles and jewellery) from Africa.

The poster would need to use the main graphic they had designed, plus the opening times etc., and was to include some images from the exhibition they had been given.

First thoughts

Sam and Dave discussed their ideas together. As before, they made a rough sketch on paper of what they wanted to achieve.

Dave opened the file that contained their original logo, without the address in the top right-hand corner.

Using the rulers they added some more guides to provide a layout grid to place their images and text on. They divided the working area of the page into six columns of 30mm. They zoomed in to make this easier to do.

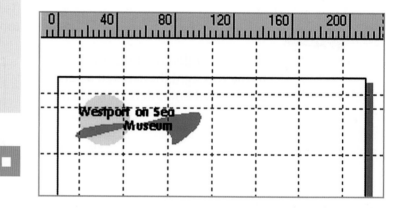

All grouped together

Sam wanted to try making the logo bigger in order to fill the top of the poster. Having clicked on the **Select** tool, she dragged the mouse across the entire logo. Then she typed `Control` + `G`. This **grouped** all the different elements (the sun, wave and text) together, so they became one object.

Next Sam re-sized the grouped selection to fill the top of the poster.

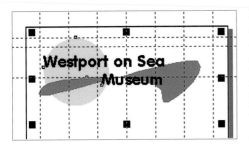

However, they decided that they didn't really like this design, so Dave typed **Control** + **Z** to undo the last action.

He then **un-grouped** the elements by keeping them selected and typing **Control** + **U**.

This time Dave just enlarged the blue wave by dragging the bottom right handle. To get the effect he wanted he then dragged the middle right handle, which stretched it across the page until it touched the right-hand margin.

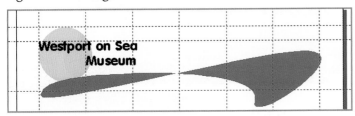

Blending in the background

Next, Sam and Dave experimented with the background **blend**. This proved more difficult than they expected, but they were surprised how much control they had. They had to experiment quite a lot to get it how they wanted.

Sam drew a rectangle that was very slightly larger than the piece of paper. Then she clicked on the **Fill** tool and the **Blend** sub-menu icon. This opened the **Fountain Fill** dialogue box.

Click here to select the colour

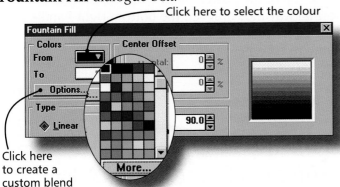

Click here to create a custom blend

She clicked on the black triangle next to the word **From**. Clicking on **More...** brought up another Fountain Fill dialogue box that she was able to change to get to the Baby Blue colour.

Then Sam clicked on **Options** to open the **Fountain Fill Color Options** box. She clicked on **Custom**.

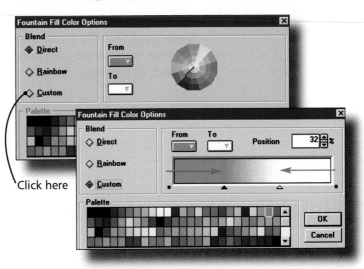

Click here

Here she moved the left-hand arrow to the right to the 32% position, and the right-hand arrow to the left to the 67% position. (See the two red arrows above). This meant that the area that would be blended would occupy the middle third of the page, and that the logo on the top would remain on a white background.

Sam pressed **OK** to close both open boxes, and the blend appeared on screen.

Keeping it selected, she needed to type **Shift** + **Page Down** to send it to the back.

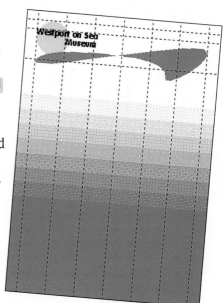

Finally, she checked what it looked like without the guides, by pressing **F9**.

WHAT YOU HAVE TO DO

Create the wider wave shape and add the blends as shown on this page.

Spend some time experimenting with the custom Fountain Fill Options box.

➡ 41

6. Creating waves

Sam and Dave's next step was to start to make their poster more eye-catching, and to decide what to do about the main title.

Finishing the background

On this page you will see how you sometimes need to approach things in different ways to get the effect you want. You will also learn about the importance of sizing and spacing of letters in titles.

Invisible circles

Sam and Dave tried to add some dark blue waves at the bottom. First of all they tried using the **Pencil** tool, but couldn't manage to create the wave shapes they wanted accurately enough. Then Sam suggested a different approach.

First she drew a 20mm high rectangular box across the bottom of the page. Then she filled it with 100% Cyan and 60% Magenta, which gave a deeper blue, and applied 'no outline'.

She added a 5mm guide line from the bottom of the page. She also made sure **Snap To Guide** (in the **Layout menu**) was ticked.

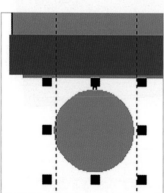

Sam drew a circle 30mm in diameter. She filled it with Baby Blue, and gave it no outline.

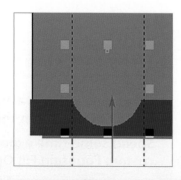

Then she moved it up onto the page, allowing it to snap to the guides exactly into position.

Sam used **Control** + **D** to duplicate the circle, and placed them along the columns.

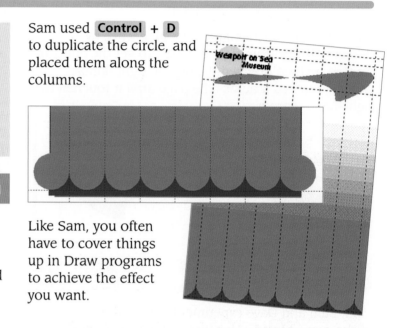

Like Sam, you often have to cover things up in Draw programs to achieve the effect you want.

The exhibition title

The next challenge was the main title. Sam and Dave decided it should be in AvanteGarde Bk BT, to match the letter-head text.

They placed the main title centrally, in the white space at the top of the poster. After entering the text in the normal way they dragged the bottom right handle to enlarge it to the size that looked best, rather than trying to set a new point size.

i Using the text roll-up window *p36* Keyboard shortcuts *p37*

Dave noticed that the letters r and t in the word 'Arts' were touching each other. He decided they needed a little more space between them. Adjusting the space between individual letters is called **kerning**.

He selected the **text** box and clicked on the **Shape** tool. He also zoomed in and added a guide to the bottom of the line of text. Now each letter had a small square handle. Using this he was able to drag the A and the r slightly to the left to make them easier to read.

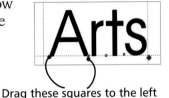

Drag these squares to the left

They created a separate text box for the words 'An exhibition of'. Remembering that every element should line up with something else, they carefully placed it to align with the bottom of the blue wave and centrally above the word 'Decorative'.

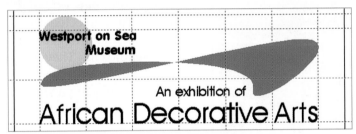

Sam copied and pasted the address text from their letter-head and positioned it bottom right, between the grid lines. She needed to add some extra information at the top and the bottom. To do this she typed **Control** + **T** to open the **Artistic Text** edit box. Here she could easily add the extra words in.

Type extra text in here

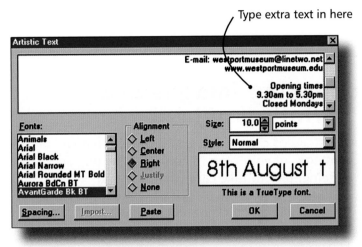

Back on the page she highlighted the dates and made them 24pt to make them easier to read from a distance.

Kerning

If certain letters are placed closely together, or too far apart in a word they can become difficult to read. Particularly with headings and titles, it is sometimes necessary to adjust the spaces between individual letters in a word. This is known as kerning.

For example the letters **WAT**
(as in the word WATER)

can be closed up **WAT**

Meanwhile the letters Illus
(as in the word Illustration)

need to be pulled apart slightly Illus

WHAT YOU HAVE TO DO

1. Take some time to see if you can work out exactly how to add the wave shape at the bottom of the poster.

2. Add the main title at the top, and the address text.

7. Pictures for an exhibition

On this page you will see how Sam and Dave carefully added clip art to the poster and printed out their final design to show the museum.

Placing images and printing out

Instead of clip art you could use alternative images of your own to complete the poster. Remember to take care when printing. It's a good idea to use a black and white printer first, which will be quicker and cheaper.

Imported pictures

Sam and Dave had been provided with a number of images of items in the exhibition that they had been told they could use. These were already in electronic format.

First they opened all the images on screen and discussed which ones they would use. They used **Import** in the **File** menu to bring them into their document.

Now they had to decide what size to make each one, and where to place it.

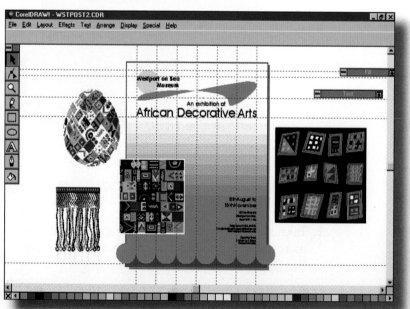

The final layout

Sam and Dave spent some time experimenting with making the images different sizes and putting them in different positions. You can see their final layout on the opposite page. Note how each image is aligned either to their original grid layout, or to the top or bottom of another element.

The image on the left was created by cropping one of the pictures. They selected the **Shape** tool and dragged the corner handles in. They also gave it a white border by creating and placing a slightly larger white box behind it.

Finally they gave the egg-shaped design a blue border. This involved using the **Outline Pen** dialogue box, which they opened by selecting the border and pressing **F12**. They set the **Width** to 1.5mm.

Print preview

Sam and Dave decided it was time to do a printout, so they could evaluate their poster design. Typing `Control` + `P` opened the **Print** dialogue box. This showed them how their design would print.

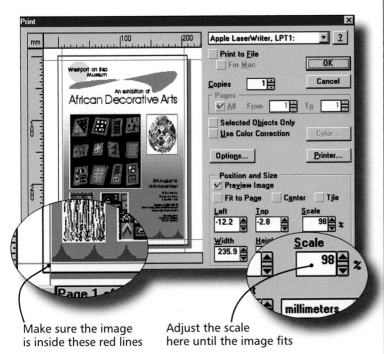

Make sure the image is inside these red lines

Adjust the scale here until the image fits

They realised that as their printer couldn't print to the edge of the paper the wave effect at the bottom would be cut off. The only way round this was to reduce the overall image to 98% and use the mouse to move it up on the page until the waves could be seen at the bottom.

Westport on Sea Museum

An exhibition of
African Decorative Arts

8th August to
15th November

18 The Parade
Westport on Sea
Kent WP1 1XU

Telephone 01234. 56789
E-mail: westportmuseum@inetwo.net
www.westportmuseum.edu

Opening times
9.30am to 5.30pm.
Closed Mondays

When they saw the printout they decided it looked fine. However, they decided to see if they could find a colour printer that would print to the edge, or onto a larger sheet of paper (e.g. A3), that they could then trim down to size.

Working in wireframe

Remember that if you have a very complex image in a **Draw** program, or your computer is not very fast, you might find it quicker to move objects around in **wireframe** (Shift + F9).

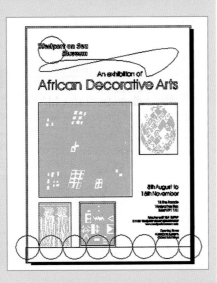

WHAT YOU HAVE TO DO

1. **Complete the poster by importing the clip art images shown. Arrange the images carefully. Print it out in colour if possible and keep it in your ICT folder. If the images shown are not available to you, go straight on to the next activity.**

2. **Import a series of different images to illustrate a different exhibition. Change the exhibition title to something more appropriate. Before you print it out discuss it with a partner.**

8. Special FX (I)

There's a lot more to Draw programs than the basic features. Here you will have a chance to experiment with some of the other tools.

The examples shown here were created by Sam and Dave. You could try copying these, or use words and shapes of your own.

Adding special effects

Sam and Dave only used the basic tools of their **Draw** program. Different Draw packages and versions offer a wide range of special effects tools. You may not have all the ones shown on this page. If this is the case, experiment with the ones you do have.

Special effects are great fun, and can add a lot of impact to your graphics. A common mistake is to get carried away and use too many at a time. As a general rule, don't use more than one special effect on any one page.

Many of the effects shown take up a lot of computer memory. Your file may very quickly get so large that it can't be copied onto a floppy disk. They can also make printing time very much slower. Always check with your teacher before printing a large graphic file.

There is not enough space here to describe all the features you can use. See if you can obtain a manual for your Draw program, or use the **Help** file to discover more about what it will do.

Filling space

Blends and patterns can be added to lettering in the same way that it can be to shapes.

Experiment with the **Fill roll-up** window. Open this from the **Fill** tool sub-menu.

Remember first to **select** the text or shape you want to apply the effect to.

Combining objects

Here the wave and sun shapes have been combined. They have both become blue, but where they overlap has become transparent.

● Select the sun. Hold down **Shift**
● Select the wave, keeping **Shift** held down
● With both items selected, press **Control** + **L** (or use **Combine** in the **Arrange** menu)

A rectangle with a spherical blend has been placed behind the image

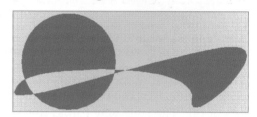

Fitting text to a path

This effect is easy to create, but quite difficult to control.

● Type a line of text
● Use the **Shape** or **Draw** tool to create a line

● **Select** the text. Hold down **Shift**
● **Select** the line
● With both items selected press **Control** + **F** (or use the **Text** menu) to bring up the **Fit Text To Path** roll-up window.

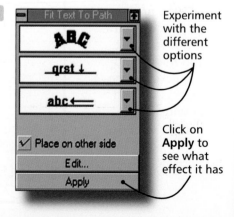

Experiment with the different options

Click on **Apply** to see what effect it has

Using the **Select** tool it is possible to edit the line or shape to improve the letter spacing along the line.

In the example shown below, the line has been given no thickness so it becomes invisible, and a yellow circle and blue rectangle have been added and sent to the back, behind the text.

Adding shadows

It's very easy to add a simple shadow to an object.

- **Select** the object. Then **duplicate** it
- Use the **Fill** tool to change the colour to a dark grey
- Drag the grey duplicate over the original, slightly off-setting it
- Use the **Arrange** menu to send the shadow to the back

In the example on the right a pale yellow rectangle has been added at the back, and given an outline colour to match the letters.

A fine outline was added to the letters to help make them stand out

Allowing the text to spill out over the background box is an effective graphic technique that helps add visual interest to a design

Envelope

The **Envelope** tool enables you to distort the shape of an object.

- Select the object (it can be a graphic, or text)
- Press **Control** + **F7** to access the **Envelope** roll-up window (or use the **Effects** menu)

Selecting the **Shape** tool gives the greatest freedom. The other boxes are useful for creating more regular shapes.

The frame round the selected object changes to a red dotted line.

The node points can now be pulled into a different shape.

- Click on **Apply** to see the effect you have created

You can make further changes to the shape until you click on the **Select** tool.

As with all special effects, it's important not to over-do it. Make sure the word can still be read easily.

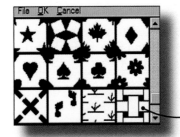

In the example shown below a rectangle has been filled with a tile from the **Fill** roll-up window

9. Special FX (2)

In the final section on using Draw packages you will see how to add three-dimensional and transparency effects to your designs.

If you are using CorelDRAW you will need to have version 6 or above to create the effects on page 49.

Add perspective ■

Adding **perspective** helps give an object a feeling of depth.

● **Select** the object
● Use the **Effects** menu and click on **Add Perspective**

The object is enclosed by a red dotted line. Pulling the nodes re-shapes the box to make it look as if the letters are receding into the background.

In the example below a different texture has been applied to the letters. A blue outline box with a similar perspective on it has also been added.

Extrude ■

The **Extrude** tool enables you to make text look three-dimensional.

● **Select** the text
● Press **Control** + **E** to bring up the **Extrude** roll-up window, or use the **Effects** menu
● Experiment with the different options

Try different extrusion depths, blends, varying the lighting, varying the letter outline thickness and revolving the object

As always, try to keep it simple! The extrusion tool is fun to use, but difficult to control to get precisely the effect you want.

A **fish-eye** lens makes a surface look like it has been covered by a large magnifying glass.

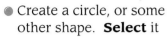

- Create a circle, or some other shape. **Select** it
- Open the **Lens** roll-up window
- Select **Fish Eye**
- Drag the shape over another object. It will enlarge the portion it covers
- Give the shape 'no outline'

You will need to experiment to get exactly the shape you want. As always, make sure any lettering can still be read.

Experiment with some of the other tools in the **Lens** roll-up window. In particular, try the **Transparency** effect. This tool makes the shapes or letters you create look like they are covered with coloured pieces of tracing paper.

In the example below a transparent circle has been added. The corners of the rectangle were rounded using the **Shape** tool.

Using the **Interactive Transparency** tool on the tool bar enables you to apply a transparency effect to text or an object and control the fade of the transparency.

In the example below the individual letters have been spaced out and moved either up or down from the base-line. This has been done using the **Shape** tool.

A transparency was then applied to the letters, and to the background. This gives the effect of the background fading out.

WHAT YOU HAVE TO DO

1. **Practise as many special effects as you can find on the Draw program you have available.**

2. **Look back at the snow-boarder poster on page 30. How many special Draw effects can you spot that have been used?**

10. It's a scan (I)

So far in this unit you have looked at ways of creating images directly on screen. Next you will see how two pupils imported existing images and then worked on them.

Getting images in

There are two main ways that images can be imported for use in a computer. One is an electronic camera, and the other is a scanner.

Once an image has been converted into a digital format it can be manipulated in special software applications. Then it can easily be placed into a poster, leaflet, etc., just like any other graphic image. Whereas **Draw** programs work with **vector** images, **Photo** programs work with **bitmap** images. You will find the basic tools similar to those found in a standard **Paint** package.

Using an electronic camera ■

The way you take a picture on a digital camera is similar to the way you use a camera with a conventional film in. What happens inside is very different however. Instead of causing a chemical reaction, the light entering the camera is converted into an electronic signal. This is stored on a special floppy disk in the camera. A computer can read this disk and therefore open the image in a drawing or photo package. The disk can then be re-used.

Digital cameras are excellent for producing 'instant' pictures. However, when using cheaper models the quality is often not very good, and they may not produce good close-up results.

It is also possible to grab images from a digital movie camera, or a VCR (although the quality is less good).

Using a scanner ■

A scanner is the best choice for digitising a 2D image up to A4 size – for example a conventionally-taken photo, or a piece of hand-made artwork.

Nathan and Arpad began by making sure the scanner was switched on and connected to the computer. They placed their original on the scanner bed as straight as possible. Then they opened the scanner software package. Nathan went to the **File** menu and clicked on **Acquire**.

A dialogue box appeared. There are many different scanning packages, so yours may look different to this one. It should have similar tools, however.

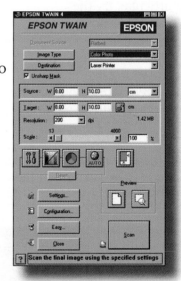

He started by clicking on **Overview**. This showed him a quick black and white 'snapshot' of what the scanner saw.

Nathan did not want the whole image so he used the red box to frame the portion of the picture he wanted.

i File formats *p14*

Next he pressed **Preview**. This showed him his selection in colour. As it was not quite right he went back and re-adjusted the red frame.

Sizing it up

At this stage Arpad needed to think about the **image size**. He had to take some decisions about the size of picture he wanted, and what quality he needed. The bigger the picture and the better the quality, the larger the file size would be. An A4 picture suitable for printing in a book or magazine might easily take up 30Mb or more – over 20 floppy disks! Meanwhile an A6 photo just to be viewed on a computer screen might be as low as 30K, which would mean that about 50 could be fitted onto one disk!

Arpad made the necessary adjustments and then clicked on **Scan**. This took a bit longer to process than the previous ones. When finished the image appeared in his photo-manipulation software package.

Then the fun began! Unlike a photo that comes back from a film-processing laboratory, changes can be made to the image before it is printed.

Size matters

The **resolution** describes the picture quality. The greater the number of ppi (pixels per inch), the better the quality. 72ppi is fine for on-screen images and produces reasonable quality prints. If you want to improve the quality try 150ppi, although this uses up four times as much memory. Good desktop printers will print images up to 300ppi. Professional print products are usually scanned at 600ppi or even 1200ppi.

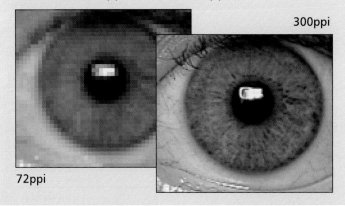

300ppi

72ppi

Light and dark

One of the first things Nathan did was to adjust the **brightness** and **contrast**. In Corel **PhotoPaint 4** this is in the **Colour** sub-menu in the **Image** menu.

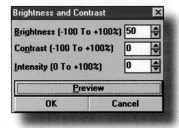

Changing the brightness made the image lighter or darker.

Increasing the contrast made the blacks blacker and the whites whiter. Decreasing it did the reverse.

11. It's a scan (2)

When you've scanned an image into your computer you can start to experiment with different filters.

Any colour you like...!

Nathan wanted to adjust the colours of the image. He opened the **Hue and Saturation** dialogue box.

Hue and Saturation ✕

Hue (-180° - +180°)

◄ ▶ 85

Saturation (-100% - +100%)

◄ ▶ -39

Preview

OK | Cancel

To change the colours of the image, he experimented with the **Saturation** slider control.

In the photograph on the bottom right, the colour is the original one. This time he adjusted the **hue** to reduce its intensity.

Using filters

Photo-manipulation software usually comes with a variety of special effect filters. Some of these filters take a while to apply. The effect can usually be previewed first.

Following are just some of the effects that can be achieved.

Pointillism

This makes the photo look like a painting by Seurat, an artist who worked in the Pointillist style in the early part of the twentieth century.

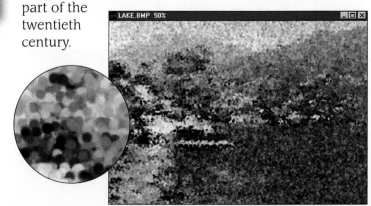

Inverse

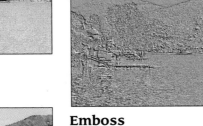

Emboss

Watercolour

Coloured pencil

Chalk and Charcoal

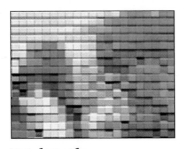

Patchwork

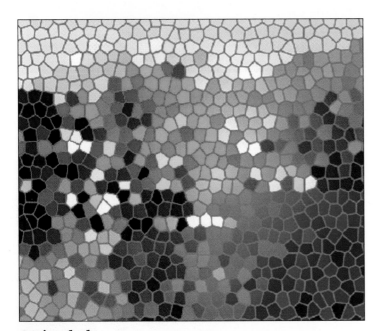

Stained glass

Touching it up

Look carefully at the photo below and compare it with the ones of the car on the left. Can you spot what's missing?

Someone appears to have removed the headlights and number plate! Of course this was done electronically.

- Zoom in on the area you want to alter
- Select the **Eye Dropper** tool and touch it on the surrounding colour
- Select the **Paintbrush** or **Spraycan** tool

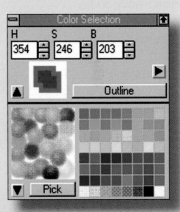

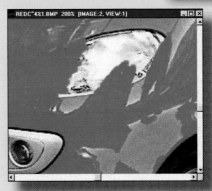

- Paint over the area you want to remove. You may want to vary the colour in places to make it look more realistic

WHAT YOU HAVE TO DO

1. Scan in a photograph. Adjust the brightness and contrast.

2. Experiment with the filters to see what effects you can achieve. For future reference, make notes of what you did, and what you thought of the results.

12. Spot the fake!

A camera never lies! But it's not difficult to alter a photograph. Sometimes it can be difficult to tell what's real.

Finally in this unit you need to find out what other image manipulation packages are available to you.

Scanning objects ■

The things you scan in don't have to be photographs. Any shallow object can be used – though ask permission first. Take great care to ensure you do not scratch the glass surface.

Adding text ■

Text can be added directly into most Photo packages. Alternatively, the image could be imported into a Draw or DTP program for further development.

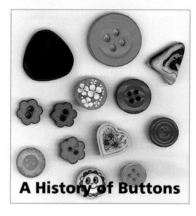

A History of Buttons

Moving and masking ■

If you look at this close-up of the bottom right-hand corner of the picture in the previous column, you'll see it's not the same.

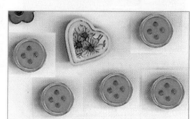

The pink button has been selected, copied and pasted over the other buttons.

Another interesting technique is **masking**. This is difficult to get the hang of and control, but with a bit of practice you should be able to have some fun moving parts of an image to different places, or other images.

Here the background of the red car photo has been masked to show only the car. Finally, below it has been pasted into the photo of the lake.

Copyright

Remember that you are breaking copyright laws if you use images from published sources (e.g. books and magazines) without permission. If it's purely for your own use it doesn't matter, but you must not re-distribute it – print it out and pass it round, give people electronic copies, or put it on the Internet.

Paint me a picture

Other similar packages to the ones you've been using are specifically for producing works of art.

These have an extensive range of pencils, pastels, brushes, etc., and also different types of paper.

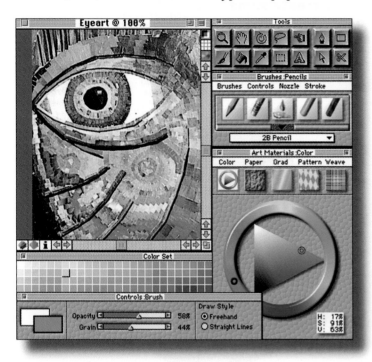

Although you can use a mouse, an electronic drawing pad will give the best results.

Into three dimensions

There are also special packages that enable you to create three-dimensional forms and landscapes.

Moving images

There is a range of software for the production of images that move. One type is for producing **animated drawings**. Another type is for editing digital **video images**. As well as simply putting a sequence of shots and sounds together, a wide variety of **fades**, **wipes** and other special effects can be added.

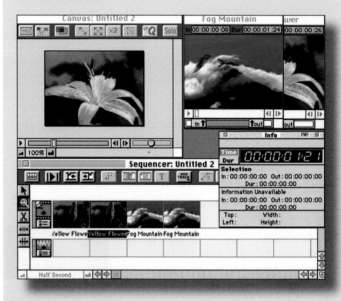

On Target

You should now know how to:

- use a wide range of tools in a drawing package
- apply some basic principles of communication design and layout
- import images into a computer and manipulate them using special software.

WHAT YOU HAVE TO DO

1. Find out more about 'masking' and the different ways it can be done.

2. Find out if you have any of the types of programs described on this page in your school.

3. Read the IT at work case study on the next page.

ELECTRONIC IMAGING

IT at work

An interview with Gary Jones, Art Production Manager at Pulse, a design and marketing company based in central London. Here he explains how he used photo-manipulation software to create some promotional material for Polaroid cameras.

The brief

'We were asked by Polaroid to create an advertisement for their SP350 camera that would appear in a trade magazine. The SP350 camera takes special Passport-sized pictures.

Polaroid supplied us with a high-resolution digital photograph of the camera and the two logos that had to be used. They also provided the text that was to appear in the advertisement, and told us the size of the space. The rest was up to us!'

approved quality
WITH SILVER HALIDE FILM

The programs

'The main program we used was called **Adobe Photoshop**. Nearly everyone uses this program, so it's known as the 'industry-standard'. It contains lots of tools and special-effect filters, such as **Distort** and **Skew**. Images can be cut out from a background, colours changed, pictures merged together into a collage, and so on.

We also used **Adobe Illustrator**, which is a vector graphics package. Things like the logos and speech boxes were done in **Illustrator**, and imported directly into **Photoshop**. The text can be added in either program.

The photograph of the woman's head and the security guard were purchased from a colour photo stock library. Once we own the rights to these pictures we can then use and alter them as we like.'

The task ■

'In **Photoshop** each part of the picture is created on its own layer. So here the camera is on one layer, the photo of the woman is on another layer, the logo is on another, the background on another, etc. The advantage of this is that changes can be made to any one element without affecting any of the others. The colour, tone or transparency of an element can be altered, or special filters applied. It also makes it easy to re-size and move the different elements as needed.

First a base colour of blue, blending to purple, was used to create the background image. The background text and other images were all given various degrees of transparency to make them fainter, so that the object in the foreground would stand out.

After the camera had been positioned, the text and other images were added. The photo of the woman's head that appears on the back of the camera needed to be skewed to make it look as if it was on the camera's view screen.'

The approval ■

'Polaroid were very pleased with the work we did on this advertisement. They felt it was visually very strong and would attract attention in the magazine. Before the final version was produced however, they asked for some changes to the text to be made. Luckily this was not difficult to do as the text was on its own layer.

After the advert had been finally approved, the images were 'flattened'. This means that the layers were all grouped into one. It was then supplied on a CD to the magazine publishers.'

WHAT YOU HAVE TO DO

Find out if the photo-manipulation program you have in school allows you to work in layers. Experiment to see what effects you can create.

INTRODUCTION

3 Desktop Publishing

In this unit you will combine text and images in a Desktop Publishing package. This will involve creating a template.

On Target

You should already know how to use a word processing package to create text documents and add images to them.

In this unit you will learn how to use desktop publishing processing software to:

- create templates for documents with more than one page
- change the appearance of the text and the layout
- save and print the work.

In this unit Microsoft **Publisher 2000** has been used. You may have a slightly different package, but you will find that all the tools are very similar. They may be located in different menus however.

Microsoft **Publisher** has many automatic **Wizard** design templates. These might help give you an idea of what can be done, but it is important that you learn how to make your own templates.

Getting on the desktop ▪

Until recently, designing a printed product was a difficult and time-consuming process. Setting type and inserting illustrations meant that it was difficult to experiment with different layouts. The terms **cut** and **paste** meant literally that – cutting strips of text up and pasting them down onto a page.

Desktop publishing (or **DTP**) has changed the way books, magazines, advertisements, etc., are created and prepared for the printer. On the computer screen it's now easy to move areas of text around, change the font and alter the size and position of a photograph or drawing. If it doesn't look right, it can be changed back in an instant.

When the design is right, it can be saved on a disk or CD and sent to the printer. Alternatively it can be sent directly over the Internet using a high-speed telephone line.

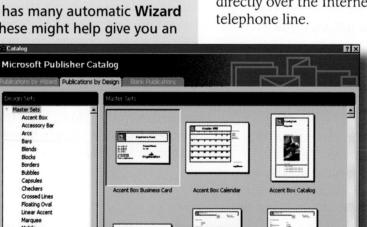

Most printed products are created by professionals who are expert in the use of DTP software and printing process technologies. However, many people in everyday life are now starting to use DTP to improve the quality of things like newsletters, promotional leaflets and greetings cards.

Desktop design

Using a DTP program is not particularly difficult. It's a bit like a more complicated word processing program. There are some new tools and techniques to learn, but you'll want to concentrate primarily on the design of the document you produce.

As always, it's essential to keep the **purpose** and **audience** for your publication firmly in mind. The style and size of lettering you choose, the illustrations and colours you use and how you organise them will all be influenced by the nature of the information you want to communicate, and the needs of the people who will be looking at it.

Use the DTP design checklist below to help you plan your publication.

DTP design checklist

Text
● Which sections of text will be used as titles and headings, main (or 'body') text, and any 'small print' captions?
● What size and style of typefaces will be most appropriate for each section?

Illustrations
● What information will be best provided by means of graphs and charts, plans, illustrative drawings, photographs, etc?
● Will artwork be clip art, specially drawn artwork or photographs?
● What size will the illustrations be?
● Will they be in colour or black and white?
● What graphic devices, i.e. lines or flat areas of colour might be effective?
● What section of text will each illustration need to be near?

Layout
● How will the text and the illustrations be best arranged for the format?

Format
● What size and type of paper will be used, and how will it be folded and/or fastened together?
● How will these decisions affect the printing and production costs?

Back to basics

Desktop publishing packages are a lot more flexible than a word processor. Basically you create a series of text boxes and picture boxes. These can be easily moved anywhere you want on the page, and over or under each other.

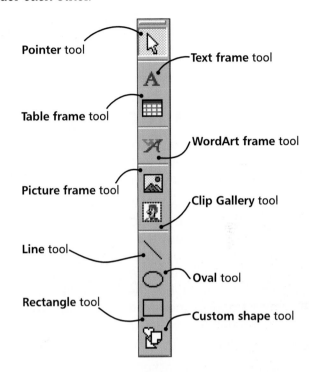

Pointer tool — Text frame tool — Table frame tool — WordArt frame tool — Picture frame tool — Clip Gallery tool — Line tool — Oval tool — Rectangle tool — Custom shape tool

Getting IT Right in...

English

DTP programs will help you produce effective project work such as newsletters and advertisements. One group of pupils designed a brochure for a holiday villa in the South of France.

Design and Technology: Graphic Products

A class were asked to design and make a calendar promoting the school. They worked together to produce a series of photos and drawings and imported them into their DTP program.

WHAT YOU HAVE TO DO

Open your DTP program. Explore the various tools and template Wizards. Make some notes about what you discover.

1. Creating the template (1)

The first step will be to create a template. This provides the structure for a publication. It can then also be used later for other similar documents.

A template is mainly created in the 'background' of a document. The content is added to the 'foreground'.

Getting the facts right

In this unit you are going to follow two pupils as they use a DTP program to create a layout for a factsheet for a local museum.

As well as their permanent collection, Westport on Sea Museum have temporary exhibitions. They are planning one about the Environment. It will have a particular focus on the design of packaging. They have prepared a draft of a free factsheet for visitors, but they would like to improve its design and layout. The improved version will then become used as a template for future factsheets.

Jane and Simon were asked to use a DTP program to develop the design. The museum wanted them to use the logo that had already been designed (see Unit 2).

First they discussed the appearance of the draft they had been given. They made the following notes:

- The sheet looked very dull and there were no graphics.
- The size of the lettering was very small.
- There were several different sizes of headings.
- There were some spelling mistakes.
- The lines of text were too long.
- The title of the sheet was not very obvious.
- There was a lot of wasted space at the bottom of the second page.
- It was difficult to tell which sheet should be read first.

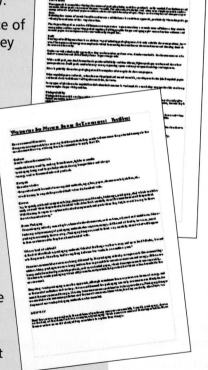

Go to Background

Jane and Simon opened **Publisher**. They immediately clicked on **Continue** in the bottom right corner to get rid of the Wizard screens and bring up a plain white page.

First they had to change the measurements from inches to centimetres. They used **Tools** and **Options** to do this.

Jane opened **Page Setup** in the **File** menu to check the size of the paper (A4 is 21 by 29.7cm). They also opened **Print Setup** to check that the paper size was set to A4 portrait.

First they needed to create a template for the factsheet that could be used for future editions. In the **View** menu they found **Go to Background**. Whatever is placed on the background will appear automatically in each new page that is inserted into a document.

Next they went to **Layout Guides** in the **Arrange** menu. They then set the left and right margins at 1.5 cm, the top margin at 2.5cm and the bottom at 2cm. They also set the number of columns they wanted at 3.

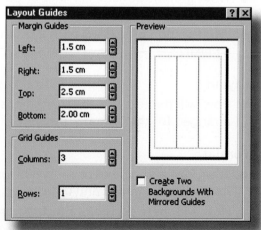

i DTP design checklist *p59* Back to basics *p59* Keyboard shortcuts *p65*

Text Frame Properties

Still in the background, Jane then used the text box tool to create a text frame. This fitted exactly over the outer pink frame guide, except at the top where it started 6cm from the top.

With the text frame highlighted, they clicked on **Text Frame Properties** in the **Format** menu, and changed the number of columns to 3. They also increased the space between the columns of text to 0.6cm.

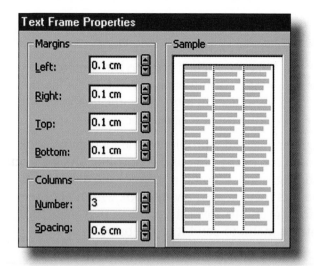

Putting on the style

The next step was to set up some **style sheets**. Style sheets pre-define a style, size and other characteristics. The specification can then be easily and quickly applied to any section of text. Jane highlighted a text frame and opened **Text Style** in the **Format** menu. Then she clicked on **New Style** and typed in the name 'Main body text'.

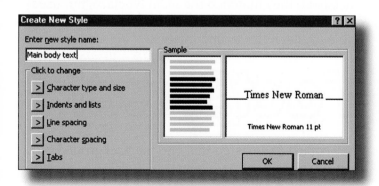

Finally, she clicked on **Character type and size**. In the dialogue box that appeared, she set the type to Times New Roman 11pt and clicked **OK**.

She repeated this process to define the 'B head' as VAG Rounded BT 14pt, and the 'C head' as the same, except at 11pt. This is the standard way in which different sizes of headings and sub-headings are categorised. There's no need to define an 'A' head, as this will be the main title.

Next Jane went up to the top left-hand corner of the tool bar and clicked on the arrow to get the style names to appear.

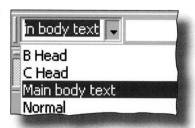

She typed in some text in a text frame and clicked on the name of the style she wanted. The text changed to the style and size she had defined.

Getting in line

Jane and Simon decided they wanted a line at the bottom of each page. Their initial idea was to have a yellow and blue line, matching the colours in the museum's logo. They drew one in using the **Line** tool, making it exactly the same width as the three columns. They held down `Shift` to keep the line horizontal.

To match the colours exactly they had to open the **Draw** file containing the museum logo and identify them as **CMYK** colours. The blue they chose was called 'Baby Blue', and they discovered it was made up of 60% Cyan and 40% Magenta. The yellow was simply 100% Yellow.

Making sure their line was highlighted they clicked on the **Line color** icon in the tool bar and selected **More color**.

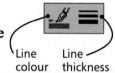

Line colour Line thickness

Then they changed the RGB box to CMYK, and typed in the percentages. When they clicked OK, the line turned the correct blue colour. Using the **Line thickness** icon, and clicking on **More Styles**, they made the line 3pt.

Next, they used the **Copy** and **Paste** commands to produce a second blue line, and repeated the above process, changing the colour to yellow (below).

2. Creating the template (2)

On the last page you learnt how to arrange the layout and how to set up the text frame properties, style sheets and line thicknesses. Next you will add page numbers, create the main heading, and complete the template.

Going dotty

Jane and Simon discussed the yellow and blue line they had created, which they thought was satisfactory, but not very interesting.

With the yellow line still selected they clicked on the **More Styles** option again and the **Dashed box**. Here they discovered some different line styles. Jane thought the circles might be fun to try, and suddenly realised this would 'echo' the circle of the logo.

They then had the idea of moving the yellow circles over the blue line. To make it work they had to go back and increase the thickness of the blue line to 10pt.

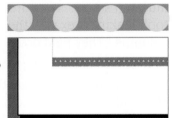

Finally, they grouped the two lines together, copied them and pasted a second set at the top of the sheet. They used the rulers to place them exactly 2cm from the top.

Page Numbers

Another element Jane and Simon wanted repeated on every page was a number. First they created a small text box in the bottom right-hand corner. Then they clicked on **Page Numbers** in the **Insert** menu.

'A #' appears in the text box. In the **foreground** this will be replaced by a sequential number on each page of the publication. They highlighted the # and changed the font to Vag Rounded BT. Finally they right-aligned it and lined the text box up carefully to the right margin.

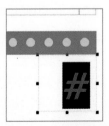

The A head

Jane and Simon switched back to the foreground (**Control** + **M**). Going back into the Draw file they imported the museum logo using the clipboard, and placed it on the top left of the sheet.

They then noticed a problem. The logo didn't look good on top of the blue and yellow line. As it was on the background, it could not simply be deleted. To solve this they created a white box with no border on the foreground to cover it up. Then they used the **Arrange** menu to send it to the back.

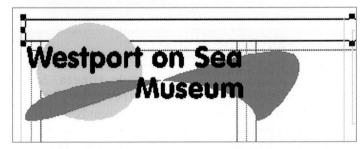

Following this, they used their **Draw** program again to create a title for the factsheet. For the word 'Factsheet' they matched the main typeface, but used an outline form. They also made the 'S' in the middle into a capital letter to add interest.

They copied and pasted this into the background of their template.

Word Art

Simon planned to use **Word Art** to create the title of the factsheet. He clicked on this icon in the tool bar and drew a text frame. Then this dialogue box appeared on screen, under the empty text frame on the screen.

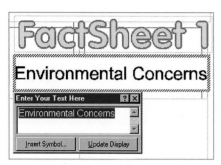

First he typed in the text he wanted and highlighted it. In the tool bar menu he selected Times New Roman for the title of the sheet, as a contrast to the VAG Rounded face.

Next, Jane clicked on the **Shadow** tool bar icon. This opened up the **Shadow** dialogue box.

She clicked on the type of shadow she thought would look best, and then on **OK**.

Finally, they wanted to make the width of the title exactly the same as the words 'FactSheet 1'. To get this right they had to adjust the amount of space between the letters.

They highlighted the title and then used the **Format** menu to open **Spacing Between Characters**. There they made the spacing 105%.

Finally, they carefully lined the bottom of the title up with the bottom of the blue shape of the logo.

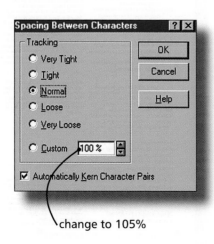

change to 105%

Turning the page

The next stage was to create the back of the sheet. First they went to **Insert** and **Insert Page**. They chose 1.

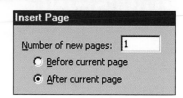

The icons shown on the right appear in the bottom left of the screen. Clicking on either page alternates between the pages.

Finishing the template

Going back to the foreground on page 2, they checked they had successfully created what they wanted.

At last they had completed their template. They chose **Save as.....Westport 1DTP** as a Publisher Template in the dialogue box.

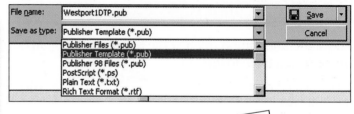

It always takes a while to set up a DTP template, but it saves a lot of time in the long run.

WHAT YOU HAVE TO DO

Follow through Jane and Simon's actions to create the template for the museum's factsheet.

3. Getting the facts down

Now the template has been created and saved, the next step is to start putting the final publication together.

Working with text

On this page you will see how the original text supplied by the museum is imported into the document and flowed across the two pages. Then you will use the style sheets to format the text.

Open the template

First Jane and Simon opened the template they had created as a new document.

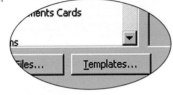

Jane clicked on the **Templates...** button on the bottom left-hand side of the **Publisher** Startup screen.

If Publisher had already been open she would have first clicked on **New** in the **File** menu to take her to the Startup screen.

When the template was open she went to the **View** menu and clicked on **Rulers** to switch them off. This gave her more space on screen to work with.

Import the text

The next thing Jane and Simon needed to do was to import the *Word* file they had been given that contained the text supplied to them by the museum.

Simon highlighted the main text frame on page 1 and chose **Text file** in the **Insert** menu.

He found the location of the *Word* file and imported it.

Alternatively, he could have opened the *Word* file, selected all the text and used the clipboard to copy and paste it into their DTP document.

Autoflow

The text flowed into the frame. When it had filled up the first page, a message appeared asking if he wanted to overflow automatically to the next page.

Simon clicked on **Yes**. He then got another message highlighting the frame on page 2, asking if he wanted to overflow to this frame. He clicked on **Yes**.

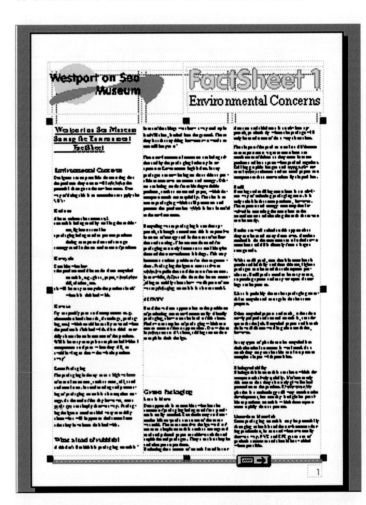

Page 1 should now look something like this

i Text frame properties *p61* Putting on the style *p61*

Back in Style

When all the text had flowed in, Simon clicked on **Control** + **A** to select all the text.

He then opened the **Style Sheet** pull-down menu, and selected **Main Body Text**.

This changed all the text into Times New Roman 11pt.

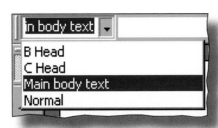

Next he deleted the previous title from the start of the text box, and clicked on each of the headings, using the **Style Sheet** menu again to make them B heads or smaller C heads.

Finally, he made the following into B heads:

● The 3Rs
● Get Packing
● Green Packaging

and all the others into C heads.

Jane noticed that although the space between the columns on page 2 was correct, the text frame on page 1 was too small. To correct this she went into **Text Frame Properties** (in the **Format** menu) and adjusted the spacing to 0.6cm.

Save IT!

Remember to save your work regularly.

Use a different name from the Template and save it as a Publisher File.

Keyboard shortcuts

Hide/Show boundaries and guides	**Ctrl** + **Shift** + **0**
Bring to front	**F6**
Send to back	**Shift** + **F6**
Zoom out to show whole page	**Ctrl** + **Shift** + **L**
Toggle between two views	**F9**
Go to background/foreground	**Ctrl** + **M**

Indents and lists

When Simon got to the second paragraph ('Reduce'), he used the bullet icon to add bullets.

He highlighted the three sentences to be bulleted and clicked on the bullet icon in the tool bar.

The bullet icon

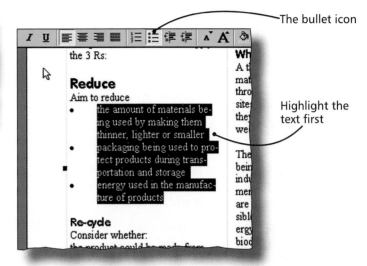

Highlight the text first

Jane and Simon decided to reduce the indent to 0.5cm by using the **Indents and Lists** window, found in the **Format** menu.

Experiment by changing these to see what happens

Change this number to 0.5cm

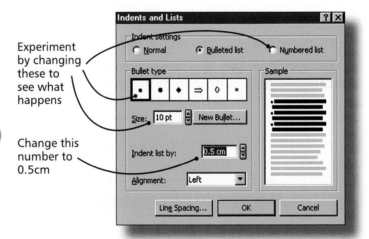

They reduced the indent size and repeated the process to create the bullets in the 'Re-cycle' paragraph.

WHAT YOU HAVE TO DO

Ask your teacher to give you a text file.

Work through the steps outlined above to import the text, change it to the correct style and to add bullets.

4. Getting in the picture (I)

Now that the text is in place it's time to put in some artwork to help bring the factsheet to life.

Adding clip art

On this page you will see how Jane and Simon added clip art to their publication. Observe how they positioned and sized the pictures they chose to help make the layout of the text work.

Instead of using clip art, they could have created their own drawings, or added photographs.

Insert clip art

Before doing any more work on the layout of the text Jane and Simon decided to choose some clip art to use as illustrations.

Jane clicked on the **Insert Clip Art** icon in the left-hand tool bar. She drew a box on the **pasteboard**. The pasteboard is the grey area around the side of the document. Anything placed here will not be printed.

She waited for the **Insert Clip Art** window to appear. In this window she typed 'Environment' into the **Search** box, and clicked anywhere on the screen.

Jane scrolled through the choices, deciding which would be the most suitable. They selected the ones they wanted by dragging the images onto the pasteboard. It takes a while for the images to copy across.

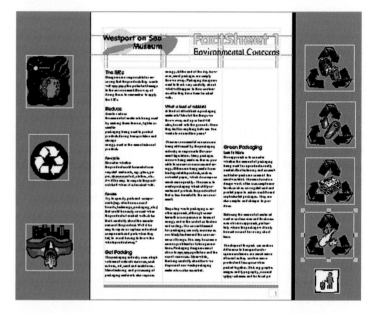

If the same images are available on your computer, find the ones they chose and drag them onto the pasteboard. If not, you will need to choose other suitable images of your own.

Finding some space

Jane dragged the image of the earth into the top left-hand corner.

Adding line spaces

Simon noticed that the text in the first column now over-ran into the second column by seven lines. He tried reducing the size of the image, but the text now appeared to its right in a very narrow column that was difficult to read.

To get round this problem, Simon added extra line spaces to push the text down below the picture until the column fitted to the bottom.

Simon experimented with different positions of the image. He decided it looked best when aligned with the right-hand edge of the first column.

Adding interest

Jane and Simon wanted the 'Green Packaging' text to start on the second page. They therefore wanted to fill the spare space on page 1 with a large image, to provide impact and variety.

Simon dragged the sewer picture to the bottom right of the page. Then he re-sized it to occupy two columns. He made sure the 'Get Packing' text did not over-run.

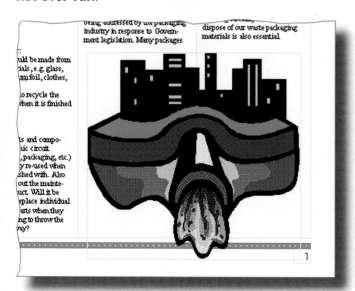

Making the sewer picture run over the base-line adds extra interest

Making it all line up

Finally, Simon added an extra line space at the top of the third column to make it align with the body text in the second column.

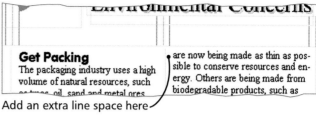

Add an extra line space here

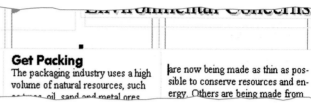

Page 1 was now complete. This is how it looked.

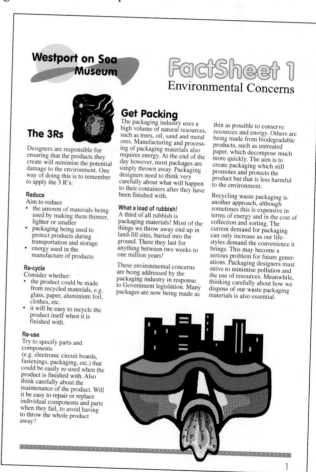

Follow Jane and Simon's actions to create your own page 1.

5. Getting in the picture (2)

Here you will complete the layout of the factsheet. One of the main advantages of using DTP is how quickly new ideas can be tried out. It only took Jane and Simon a few minutes to try a completely different layout.

Turning the page

Jane and Simon then turned to page 2.

They placed the black recycling logo in the top left-hand corner. Jane re-sized it to fill a column width.

To get it to go to the top of the column, Jane had to crop the top of the frame, using the crop tool.

the **crop** tool

Simon then deleted the extra line spaces to bring the 'Green Packaging' text to the top of the column.

They moved the image down slightly to fall in between the two titles.

At the bottom of the column they inserted the picture of the tin can and battery. As they dragged the image over, it went behind the text frame. Keeping the image highlighted they pressed **F6** to bring it to the front.

Jane placed the image with the glass bottle under the fourth paragraph in the second column which is about glass. They added an extra space to the bottom of the column to move the next heading 'Biodegradability' to the top of the third column.

The picture with the newspapers was then placed after the first paragraph in the third column. Note how these three pictures form a diagonal line across the page.

Finally, they added the picture of a person throwing their rubbish away at the end of the text, in the bottom right-hand corner. This made a good end to the sheet.

Green Packaging

Less is More
One approach is to consider whether the amount of packaging being used for a product is really needed. Confectionary and cosmetics blister-packs are some of the most wasteful. The most creative design work often uses simple materials such as corrugated card and printed paper to achieve subtle and sophisticated packages. They are also simpler and cheaper to produce.

Reducing the amount of material used in surface area and thickness is an obvious approach, particularly where the package will only be used once of for a very short time.

The shape of the pack can make a difference to transport costs – square containers are much more efficient as they contain more product and less space when packed together. Striking graphic images and typography, unusual colour schemes and textured papers can compensate for a conventionally shaped box.

Glass is probably the easiest packaging material to recycle and use again for the same purpose.

Often recycled papers and cards, rather than newly pulped and treated materials, are adequate for the job. Recycled papers and boards do have different working characteristics, however.

Many types of plastic can be recycled but their chemical structure is weakened. As a result they may not be able to take up more complex shapes with precision.

Refill
Reusing and refilling containers is an obvious way of reducing packaging costs. It is only suitable for some products, however. The expense and energy consumption involved in returning the container to the manufacturer and cleaning them fit for re-use can be costly.

Bottles are well suited to this approach as they can be used many times over. Another method is for the consumer to take their own container and fill it directly from a larger storage unit.

With a refill pack, one durable container is purchased initially and then thinner, lighter packages can be used for subsequent purchases. Refill packs need to be easy to use, so pouring spouts and easy-to-open fastenings are important.

Biodegradability
Biodegradable materials are those which decompose relatively quickly. Unfortunately this means that they also only give limited protection to the product. Biodestructable plastics is a technology still very much under development, but one day it might be possible to produce materials which decompose more rapidly than at present.

Hazardous Materials
Some packaging materials may be potentially damaging to health and the environment during production, in use and when eventually thrown away. PVC and CFC gases are of particular concern and should be avoided where possible.

Litter
Reducing the number of separate parts in a package helps reduce the possibility of them being 'dropped' rather than thrown away. One familiar, but now solved, problem is that of the can ring-pull. How has this been solved?

Packaging designers need to graphically remind and prompt users to throw packaging materials away properly.

2

The completed page 2

 DTP design checklist p59

All change

Jane and Simon wondered if the factsheet might be even better if it were designed as a three-fold brochure. They used exactly the same words and pictures but experimented by changing:

- the page format (to landscape)
- the text styles
- the layout of the text and images.

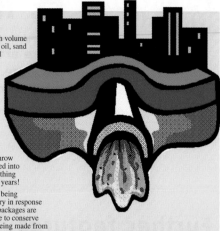

The 3Rs

Designers are responsible for ensuring that the products they create will minimise the potential damage to the environment. One way of doing this is to remember to apply the 3 R's:

Reduce

Aim to reduce
- the amount of materials being used by making them thinner, lighter or smaller
- packaging being used to protect products during transportation and storage
- energy used in the manufacture of products

Re-cycle

Consider whether:
- the product could be made from recycled materials, e.g. glass, paper, aluminium foil, clothes, etc.
- it will be easy to recycle the product itself when it is finished with.

Re-use

Try to specify parts and components (e.g. electronic circuit boards, fastenings, packaging, etc.) that could be easily re-used when the product is finished with. Also think carefully about the maintenance of the product. Will it be easy to repair or replace individual components and parts when they fail, to avoid having to throw the whole product away?

Get Packing

The packaging industry uses a high volume of natural resources, such as trees, oil, sand and metal ores. Manufacturing and processing of packaging materials also requires energy. At the end of the day however, most packages are simply thrown away. Packaging designers need to think very carefully about what will happen to their containers after they have been finished with.

What a load of rubbish!

A third of all rubbish is packaging materials! Most of the things we throw away end up in land-fill sites, buried into the ground. There they last for anything between two weeks to one million years!

These environmental concerns are being addressed by the packaging industry in response to Government legislation. Many packages are now being made as thin as possible to conserve resources and energy. Others are being made from biodegradable products, such as untreated paper, which decompose much more quickly. The aim is to create packaging which still promotes and protects the product but that is less harmful to the environment.

Recycling waste packaging is another approach, although sometimes this is expensive in terms of energy and in the cost of collection and sorting. The current demand for packaging can only increase as our lifestyles demand the convenience it brings. This may become a serious problem for future generations. Packaging designers must strive to minimise pollution and the use of resources. Meanwhile, thinking carefully about how we dispose of our waste packaging materials is also essential.

Green Packaging

Less is More

One approach is to consider whether the amount of packaging being used for a product is really needed. Confectionery and cosmetics blister-packs are some of the most wasteful. The most creative design work often uses simple materials such as corrugated card and printed paper to achieve subtle and sophisticated packages. They are also simpler and cheaper to produce.

Reducing the amount of material used in surface area and thickness is an obvious approach, particularly where the package will only be used once of for a very short time. The shape of the pack can make a difference to transport costs – square containers are much more efficient as they contain more product and less space when packed together. Striking graphic images and typography, unusual colour schemes and textured papers can compensate for a conventionally shaped box.

Refill

Reusing and refilling containers is an obvious way of reducing packaging costs. It is only suitable for some products, however. The expense and energy consumption involved in returning the container to the manufacturer and cleaning them fit for re-use can be costly.

Bottles are well suited to this approach as they can be used many times over. Another method is for the consumer to take their own container and fill it directly from a larger storage unit. With a refill pack, one durable container is purchased initially and then thinner, lighter packages can be used for subsequent purchases. Refill packs need to be easy to use, so pouring spouts and easy-to-open fastenings are important.

Glass is probably the easiest packaging material to recycle and use again for the same purpose. Often recycled papers and cards, rather than newly pulped and treated materials, are adequate for the job. Recycled papers and boards do have different working characteristics, however. Many types of plastic can be recycled but their chemical structure is weakened. As a result they may not be able to take up more complex shapes with precision.

Biodegradability

Biodegradable materials are those which decompose relatively quickly. Unfortunately this means that they also only give limited protection to the product. Biodestructable plastics is a technology still very much under development, but one day it might be possible to produce materials which decompose more rapidly than at present.

Hazardous Materials

Some packaging materials may be potentially damaging to health and the environment during production, in use and when eventually thrown away. PVC and CFC gases are of particular concern and should be avoided where possible.

Litter

Reducing the number of separate parts in a package helps reduce the possibility of them being 'dropped' rather than thrown away. One familiar, but now solved, problem is that of the can ring-pull. How has this been solved? Packaging designers need to graphically remind and prompt users to throw packaging materials away properly.

Westport on Sea Museum

FactSheet 1
Environmental Concerns

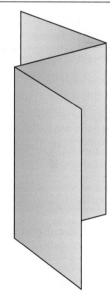

Jane and Simon found it difficult to decide which version they thought was best. Which do you think is the most successful?

Hard copy

When Jane and Simon were happy with their final design they printed it out to show the museum for their approval. As well as the two full-colour sheets they used a photocopier to produce a black and white version with both sides printed back to back.

WHAT YOU HAVE TO DO

1. Follow the steps Jane and Simon took to create the second page of their factsheet.

2. Use sketches and notes to suggest some other ways in which the layout could be done in a completely different way.

6. More dialogue

There are many other things you can do in a DTP package. On these final pages you can experiment with some of them.

Further features

Although Jane and Simon used most of the basic DTP tools while they were creating their factsheet, there were several that they did not find a use for. These are described on this page. You will also find many more tools and dialogue boxes in addition to the ones described here. Some you will find easy to work out for yourself with a little experimentation. You may find it helpful to use the **Help** file.

DTP packages like Microsoft **Publisher** are very similar to the ones used by professionals. If you ever have the chance, try Adobe **In Design**, Adobe **PageMaker**, or **QuarkXpress**. If you have mastered **Publisher**, you may be surprised at how easy you find them.

Line spacing

From the **Line Spacing** dialogue box (in the **Format** menu) you can change the space between lines, and between paragraphs. This can often be very useful, particularly when space is tight, or you want to make the text easier to read.

Experiment to find out what works best for the document you are working on. As a general rule don't add too much space, or make the lines too close together.

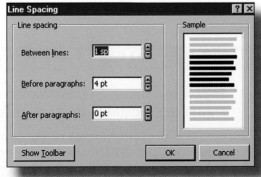

Linking text frames

In the picture below there are three faint text frames. The first contains some text, but the other two are empty.

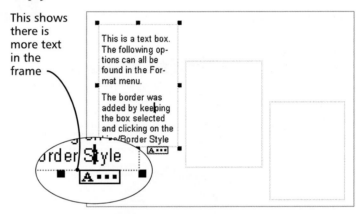

There is more text in the first frame than can be fitted in. This can be 'overflowed' into the next frame.

● Click on the **Connect Frames** icon

The mouse pointer becomes a 'jug' full of extra text.

Clicking in an empty text frame pours the words in.

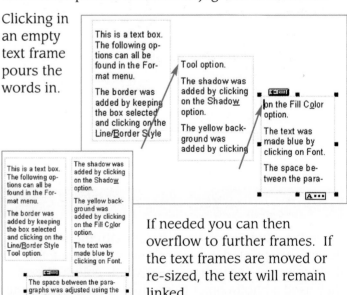

If needed you can then overflow to further frames. If the text frames are moved or re-sized, the text will remain linked.

On the table

Tables are very easy to create in **Publisher**. Click on the **Table** icon, and draw a rectangle – a dialogue box will appear giving you a range of ready-made styles of table to choose from. You can always re-size and adjust them later if necessary. When you click **OK** the table will appear on screen, ready for you to type into.

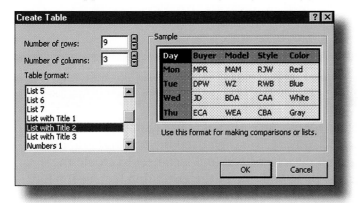

Experiment by dragging these lines to discover how to adjust the size of the table

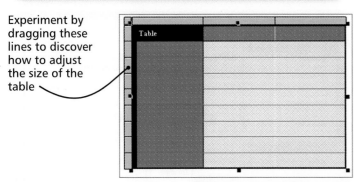

Double-page spreads

If you are creating a document that will contain left and right pages you may find it helpful to be able to see both pages at once. This is known as a 'double-page spread'.

Simply click on **Two Page Spread** in the **View** menu.

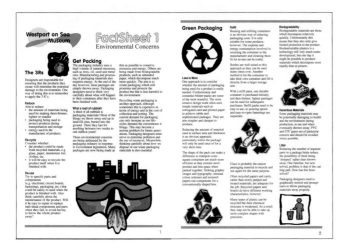

Text wrap

You will probably be familiar with the idea of **text wrap** from your word processing package. In **Publisher** you'll find you have more control over the 'wrap'.

- Click on the **Picture Frame** Tool and draw a rectangle
- Insert a picture
- Drag the picture to position in a text box

The text on the left-hand side is wrapped to the left-hand edge of the picture frame.

- With the picture selected, click on the **Custom Text wrap** tool and then the **Node** tool
- Press `Control` and position the cursor on the picture frame where you want to add an **Adjust Handle**. Then click
- Drag the black handles to pull the Picture frame in closer to the object. The text will then wrap round the picture more closely

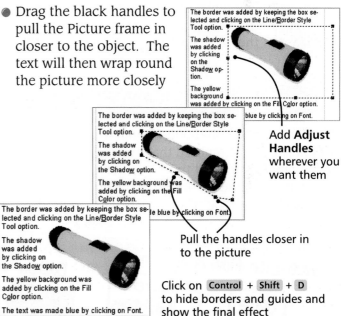

Node

Text wrap

Add **Adjust Handles** wherever you want them

Pull the handles closer in to the picture

Click on `Control` + `Shift` + `D` to hide borders and guides and show the final effect

Custom Shapes

Click on the **Custom Shapes** icon in the left-hand tool bar, and then on one of the shapes that appear. If you now draw a frame on the page, it will be the shape you selected.
Use **line** and **color** in the usual way.

Custom shape

7. Create Underline{W}eb site

Many DTP programs now have a feature that you can use to design a web site instead of using a web editor.

If you look in the File menu of later versions of Microsoft *Publisher* you will find an option called Create Web site from Current Publication.

Working on the web

In many DTP packages you can also create web sites. Some will create one based on a printed publication you've prepared, though it's best to start from scratch, perhaps using a template **Wizard**.

Jane and Simon decided to have a go at creating a web site for Westport on Sea museum, using a Wizard in their DTP package.

First thoughts

First Jane and Simon thought about a design for their overall site. They realised that different visitors would be looking for different things, so they grouped certain page types together to appeal to the audience they were likely to attract. They sketched out their ideas on paper first.

Web site Wizard

From the Wizard template menu Simon selected one called 'Waves'. He then used the text and graphics from their letter-head and factsheet to create the home page and one of the exhibition factsheet pages.

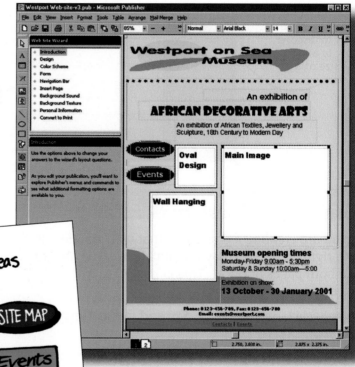

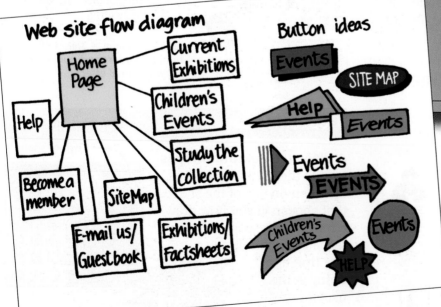

Moving around

Making it easy for users to navigate their way around a web site is very important. Colourful or unusual buttons can help make links easier to recognise.

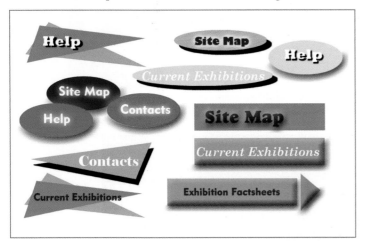

Jane and Simon found working on the web much more limiting than designing something to be printed, but managed to find some ways around the problems they encountered. They found it useful to follow the checklist below.

Remember you can preview your web site in your Internet browser.

Web site design checklist

- Is the information logically organised?
- Is there a consistent navigation structure, with a minimum of simple buttons and links in the same place on each page?
- Is there plenty of space on each page?
- Are there any attractive or unusual graphics – possibly an animation?
- Will each page not take too long to download? Are they less than 40 to 50 Kb each? To keep them small try to use images more than once, keep text and graphics separate and keep text plain to avoid it becoming a graphic.
- Have tabs, indentation, kerning and non-standard line spacing been avoided?
- Is colour used to provide subtle backgrounds? Use one particular colour only for links.
- Are the fonts used common ones such as: Arial, Arial Black, Comic Sans, Courier New, Georgia, Impact, Symbol, Times New Roman, Trebuchet and Verdana?
- Has the amount of text on each screen been kept to a minimum? About 100 to 150 words is a good guide, unless the page scrolls downwards.

On Target

You should now know how to use desktop publishing processing software to:

- create templates for documents with more than one page
- change the appearance of the text and the layout
- save and print the work.

WHAT YOU HAVE TO DO

1. **Experiment with the tools and features described on pages 70 to 73.**
2. **Save your files and make notes about what you discovered to put into your ICT folder.**
3. **Read the IT at work case study on the next page.**

IT at work

Carla Turchini works as a freelance designer. She uses a desktop publishing system to create educational and promotional materials for a variety of clients.

GRAPHICDESIGN

How it all starts

'One of my commissions was to design a series of books for the British Museum. These were on the theme of Myths and Legends.

I was told a number of things that had already been decided. These were that:

- they were aimed at children
- the size of each page was to be 240 by 171mm
- there could be one picture per double-page spread
- there would be 48 pages altogether.

They provided all the text and the pictures.

I was also asked to design the covers, and the different logos that went on each one.'

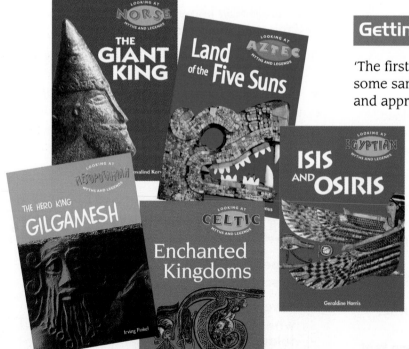

Getting the template right

'The first stage was to create a template and produce some sample spreads for the British Museum to check and approve.

For the main body text I chose 'New Aster'. This is a serif typeface which is easy to read where there is a lot of text. Some sections of text were placed in boxes with coloured tints. A slightly smaller size of the same typeface was used in these.

The main headings varied in each book. I chose a more decorative typeface that was appropriate to the particular topic of the book.

When the basic design had been finalised I began to put each book together. The whole process takes three or four months from the time I start to when I hand the finished version to the printer.'

Putting it all together

'I bring in the text files and the images and arrange them on each page. Although there is an underlying grid for margins and column widths, I have to think about the design of each page individually.

I often have to make corrections to the text as required by the editor. Usually I print the pages out so that they can be checked, but I sometimes supply them as electronic files that can be sent immediately over a high-speed ISDN telephone line.

When everything is right I 'burn' the files onto a CD, ready for the printer, but if there's a rush I sometimes have to ISDN them. This costs a lot, but it's a very quick and efficient way of sending them anywhere in the world in just a few minutes.'

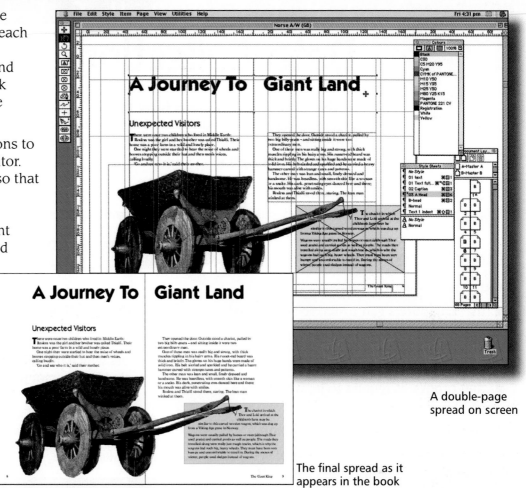

A double-page spread on screen

The final spread as it appears in the book

The advantages, and disadvantages

'Working with a computer has many advantages. In the 1980s I literally used to cut up the text into sections and paste it down onto each page. It was very time consuming to do any corrections. Also it took ages to mark up a photograph to show exactly what size it should be, how it should be cropped, and where it should be placed. Now I can do all this in seconds, and spend some time experimenting to get the best results.

There are some disadvantages too though! My clients know it's easier for me to make changes, so they are always asking me to re-do things, and we now need more proof stages. They also expect me to be able to get things done more quickly !'

My computer

'The computer system I use is an Apple Macintosh G3. Most people in publishing use Macs. The DTP program I use is called QuarkXpress. I also use Photoshop to work on the images, and I have a Linotype scanner. The logos are created in Illustrator, which is a professional vector drawing package.'

4

Data Collection

In this unit you will learn how to use a computer to sense physical data and log results. The information you collect will need to be presented effectively so your results can be shared with others.

On Target

You should already know:

- that computers can be linked to external devices
- that computers can be programmed to undertake tasks at set intervals
- that programs require to be written in a certain way.

In this unit you will go on to learn about:

- how to sense changes in physical systems such as heat, light, sound and movement
- designing a system to collect and store the resulting data
- using computers to analyse and present the data in various ways
- the benefits of using computers to sense and record physical changes.

An automatic weather station uses **sensors** to collect data without the need for anyone to be there. You can find out more about this towards the end of the unit.

Making sense of the world

Physical changes such as temperature, light, sound and movement are measured with instruments such as thermometers, light and sound meters. Changes in our environment can be monitored using electronic sensors which produce electrical signals that can be detected by a computer.

A range of sensors from the LogIT system, including temperature, air pressure, light, sound, and humidity. You can also see a pair of light gates as well as voltage, magnetic flux and temperature probes

A LEGO Dacta® touch sensor

A LEGO Dacta® angle and rotation sensor

A LEGO Dacta® temperature sensor

A LEGO Dacta® light sensor

i IT at work *p86* Sensors *p91* Using data collection skills *p138*

Computers are often used to sense changes in physical systems because they can carry out work which is either exceedingly repetitive or in hostile surroundings. For example, an incubator for premature babies can monitor the temperature, heart rate, breathing rate, oxygen saturation and blood pressure. This allows a nurse to look after several babies at the same time.

It would be very expensive to pay someone to watch each baby all the time.

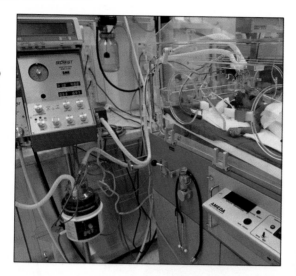

Some tasks would be impossible without the remote sensing capabilities of modern technology. The exploration of another planet or providing a continual flow of weather data from remote locations out at sea or on the top of a mountain are some examples.

The Mars Polar Lander

Some computers use sensors to help them control the conditions around them. For example, a central heating system will sense the room temperature and turn the heating on and off to keep the house warm. More sophisticated examples are found in commercial greenhouses where temperature, light and humidity are closely monitored to provide the ideal conditions for growing plants.

Getting IT Right in...

Geography
A class used weather and pollution data for topics about climate and the environment. Some pupils undertook a virtual geography field trip on the internet.

Science
Pupils logged the results of an experiment and the shared the data with other local schools. They compared their results with those from the other schools to see if the outcomes were the same.

Food Technology
A team of pupils assessed the merits of different containers to keep a meal hot using a heat sensor that recorded the temperature over a certain length of time.

Sensors are used to diagnose the settings of a car engine so that it can be tuned to control the exhaust gases to comply with the law.

You will be using sensors as part of a control system in Unit 5.

WHAT YOU HAVE TO DO

1. Make a list of different types of sensors with examples of their uses.

2. Explain the benefits of using computers for remote sensing.

3. Discuss any problems that may arise.

I. Making sense of it all

First you need to learn more about sensors, and how they can be connected to a computer.

Do you know the difference between an analogue and a digital signal?

Sensing change

On this page you will learn how computers can be made to sense changes in the physical environment and store the results. It is important that you understand the difference between analogue and digital sensors.

You will be using a number of different sensors to make things happen in Unit 5.

Setting up the hardware ■

The equipment available differs between schools, but most systems use some kind of **interface**, sometimes known as a buffer or interface box. This box takes the voltage signal from a sensor and changes it to an electrical signal the computer can respond to.

A LEGO Dacta® RCX interface. You can see three sensors at the top: light, touch and temperature. In addition to monitoring and logging data from these and a selection of the LogIT range of sensors, the RCX can also control outputs such as the motors and lamp shown.

LogIT LIVE. This interface, seen in the foreground, is transferring data from the two light gates in real-time to the computer. On the screen you can see the times taken by the trolley to pass from one light gate to the second.

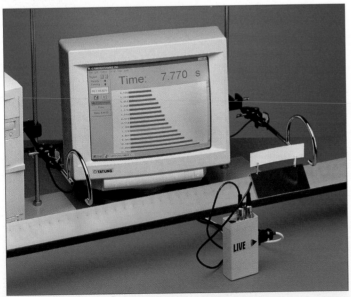

Time: 7.770 s

A LogIT DataMeter 1000. This interface has a memory to store data away from computers. When linked to a computer it can upload a number of previously recorded experiments, or run in real-time.

Analogue or digital?

Some of the devices that can be attached to the interface box are **digital**. They produce a signal that is either **on** or **off**. For example, inputs such as a push switch or pressure pad, run through the interface, and can be detected by the computer.

Interface boxes sometimes have separate **analogue input ports**. Analogue signals change continuously. Devices such as temperature, light or sound sensors detect changes which are analogue in their form. The interface box converts these analogue electrical signals into digital, 'on or off' pulses that the computer can process. This is the process that is used to turn sound signals (analogue) into digital pulses that can be stored on a music CD.

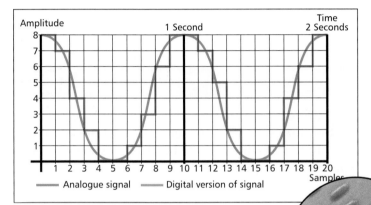

Diagram of analogue signal from a sound sensor sampled into digital pulses

Analogue devices	Digital devices
Light dimmer	Barcode
Sun dial	Digital watch
Loudspeaker	Pressure pad
Thermostat	Bell push
Spring balance	Light gate
Joystick	

Lighting the way

The pupils in a class were considering how the street lights worked outside the school. In the evening it gets dark and the lights turn on. As it gets lighter in the morning, they turn off.

The pupils decided to build a model to copy this. They used a light sensor and a lamp. They regulated the light in the room to see if the lamp would turn on when it got dark.

Storing digital data

A CD-ROM contains a spiral track of minute pits. The pits represent zeros, the surface represents the ones. The pits are non-reflective and as such can be read by a laser beam.

A CD-ROM can contain about 650Mb of digital data, but a DVD can store up to 17Gb of data – equivalent to 26 CD-ROMS.

WHAT YOU HAVE TO DO

1. **What further examples of analogue and digital devices can you think of?**

2. **Which of the following sensing devices are analogue, and which are digital?**
   - A moisture sensor.
   - A light sensor.
   - A temperature sensor.
   - A thermal switch.
   - A movement sensor.
   - A push switch.
   - A pressure sensor.

   Draw up and complete a table similar to the one on the left.

2. Collecting the data

Here you will see how two pupils used a program that allowed the computer to record or log the results from sensors.

Data logging

On this page you will:

- learn how electronic sensing can collect data in an experiment
- consider the advantages and disadvantages of using computer sensors to measure the results.

Getting into hot water

Terry and Julie, two pupils in a Food Technology class were asked to investigate the different ways that food could be kept hot. They collected different kinds of packaging from fast food restaurants and roadside cafés.

They decided to test the effectiveness of different hot drink containers. They had a china mug, a polystyrene cup and a plastic cup with a lid.

By recording the temperature of the drink over 15 minutes, Terry and Julie could find out which one kept the drink hottest.

- What would they have to do to make sure that the test is a fair one?
- What factor could they keep the same in each test?

Taking the temperature

Their first task was to record the temperature. Temperature sensors were set up so that they could be put into the hot drinks. The teacher provided the hot water for the experiment.

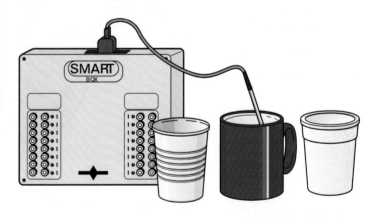

Running the experiment

While the experiment ran, the computer recorded the temperature as often as it had been instructed. At set intervals the computer read the values from the sensor and stored the figure in its memory.

Into the cool

When the experiment ended the data was saved as a file on a disk to be processed later. The software the pupils used produced a real-time graph as it took the reading, so they could watch the temperature falling. When the 15 minutes were up the computer displayed the reading as a table and offered the chance to view the results as a bar chart or a line graph.

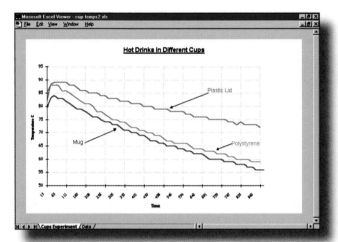

- In which container did the drink cool fastest?
- What was the initial reading when the computer began to take readings?
- Why do you think the temperature of the water in each container was not identical at the start?
- Does it make a difference to the results?
- How could the pupils be more confident of their results?

Controlling the readings

It is possible to control the readings taken by the computer. If you use a control system such as **Logicator** then the control flow chart would look something like this.

- How often would the computer above take readings?
- How many readings would it take in 15 minutes?

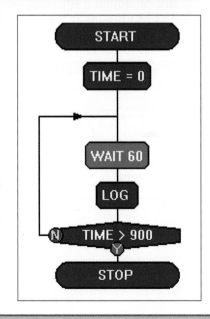

IT at work

Sensing and storing data is one of the most common applications for computers. For example:

- in science for reading signals from space,
- in banking for reading and sorting cheques,
- in town centres for measuring traffic flows or pollution levels.

Computers are ideally suited for this kind of work. Indeed, many of these kinds of applications would be impossible without the development of micro-computer technology.

Air traffic conrollers need constantly up-dated information about the position, altitude and speed of the aircraft that are taking off and landing. This data is recorded for later analysis in cases of near-misses and more serious accidents.

WHAT YOU HAVE TO DO

1. Work through the same experiment as Terry and Julie, using whatever hardware and software are available in your school.

2. Terry and Julie were interested in the importance of the lid. How would you test the effect the lid had on the temperature of the drink? Design and conduct an experiment to show this.

3. What alternative to using electronic sensors could you use?

4. What are the advantages of getting the computer to record the data in the cooling experiment?

3. Data or information?

On this page you will learn the difference between data and information, and how the pupils' results collected by the experiment were analysed and displayed.

Manipulating the data

You have seen how a computer can detect physical changes and store the results. Typically the data will be saved as a series of numbers separated by commas. However, as such they are not much use, because on their own they have no meaning. **Data** has to be converted into **information**. **Tables** or **graphs** tell us the meaning of what has been recorded.

Use a spreadsheet ■

Data logging software can store the readings from the sensors as a **.csv** file (**comma separated variables**). In the cooling experiment the variable was the temperature. This type of file can be imported into a spreadsheet.

Terry and Julie decided to use a spreadsheet like **Excel** to read the data they had collected. This is because **Excel** offers more graphing options than the data logging software. Choosing the right chart helps to give meaning to the data because a picture can make it easier to understand and make comparisons.

Terry opened a data file. He needed to 'tell' **Excel** that the file had a .csv file ending. The data was displayed in columns with the time in the first column and the temperature recorded in the second.

To make a chart from this he first selected the data by using **Shift** and any of the arrow keys on the keyboard. Then he used the **Chart Wizard** to take him through the process of making a chart

Finally, he added a title and label to his chart. **Excel** needed to know that the data was in columns and that the first column was to be used as the x-axis.

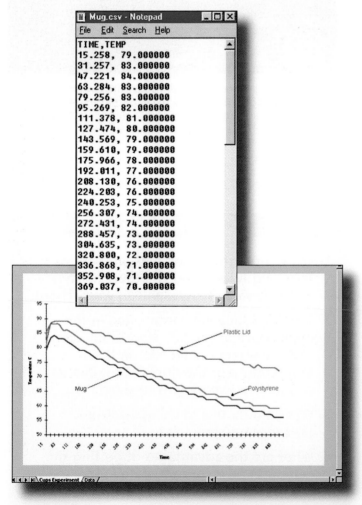

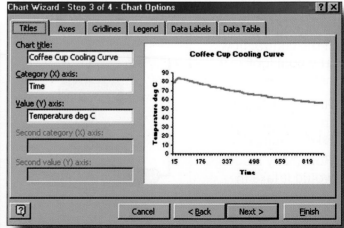

Julie then combined the data collected from the different types of mug on the same table by pasting the columns from other files. Then she could display the three types of containers on the same graph.

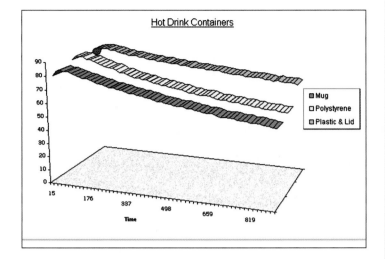

Julie tried different types of chart. She experimented with lines, markers and labels and looked at possible 2-D or 3-D views for their chart.

● What do you think are the most appropriate types of graph for this experiment?

She printed out two types of graph that she thought a reader would understand and kept them in her ICT folder. She added notes to explain which she thought would be the better one to use, and why.

Getting the temperature just right

Although Terry and Julie now had the information displayed in their charts it still did not give the whole story. They needed to find out what temperature was too hot or too cold for the drink and add this information to their chart so that they could find out which container kept the drink hot enough for the longest time.

To do this they had to test the drinks themselves at different temperatures and carry out a survey. They could mark on their charts the point where the drink became too cold. They did this using the drawing and labelling features of the spreadsheet software.

WHAT YOU HAVE TO DO

1. **Finish off Terry and Julie's experiment as described on this page.**

2. **Collect different types of chart from newspapers. Make a list of the different chart types and examples of how they can be used.**

3. **Imagine you are a manufacturer of drinks cartons. Use DTP or a presentation package such as PowerPoint to create a presentation for a take-away chain trying to choose the best type of container. Consider using the following:**

   - **a graph to compare the different mugs**
   - **a word processor or the text functions in Excel to type up the details of the experiment and the analysis of the results**
   - **a digital camera to take pictures of the experiment.**

   Decide the most appropriate way to combine and present all of the information.

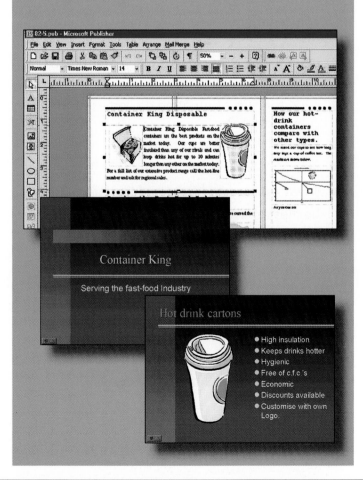

4. Public information systems

On the final page of this unit you will see that the information you have collected can be shared either within the school, or with pupils in other schools.

Sharing information

Information is of little value unless other people can receive and understand it. When you prepare information for the public it is important to consider the needs of your potential audience. This often requires investigation to discover things such as:

- how much they already know
- what makes the information interesting to them
- how they might react
- how they can pass on their response.

Of course different people will have different needs.

As you prepare the information, you also need to think about the following:

- what specific information do you want to communicate?
- how much detail is needed?
- why do you want to communicate it?
- when, where and how could the information be most effectively communicated?

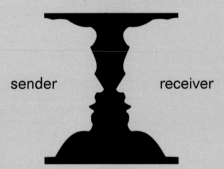

sender   receiver

Before you work though this page, read through *IT at work* on pages 86-87.

When the rain comes

Weather forecasting has become more accurate because the data available comes from a number of sources. Remote sensing of weather data provides more reliable information for farmers, travellers, sports people and the general public to plan for the weather.

A pupil collected examples for a day of when, how and for whom the weather is reported. He included the following:

- Teletext/Ceefax
- Internet
- Telephone
- Television
- Local weather data
- Readings taken at school using sensors.

What data is it necessary to record in order to describe the weather accurately?

What sensors are needed to take these readings?

A LogIT DataMeter 1000 recording water temperature using the ProTemp probe. A wide range of different sensors, eg., light and humidity, can also be used to monitor and log the environment

Communicating

One of the changes brought about by the introduction of the Internet into schools is that information generated by one class can be shared with other people.

For example, within the school it would be possible to create a rolling presentation for the foyer or a parents' evening using a presentation package such as **PowerPoint**. Alternatively, if the school has an automatic weather station these results can be displayed on their web site.

Other schools in a different area could do the same and then they could compare the results. This can also be done with schools in other countries, as the information can be seen by anyone once it has been posted on the Internet.

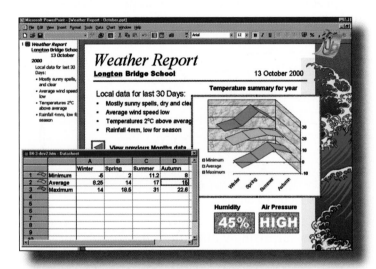

Look at the screenshot above. It shows a web template for a summary of the weather during a month. Which data has to be changed or updated each month?

On Target

You should now know:

- how to sense changes in physical systems such as heat, light, sound and movement
- how to design a system to collect and store the resulting data
- how to use computers to analyse and present the data in various ways
- the benefits of using computers to sense and record physical changes.

Using a web editor it is relatively easy to edit the page, adding in new information. For example, a weather summary could include average, minimum and maximum temperature and rainfall for each month. Once calculated, the information stored in the page can be easily updated.

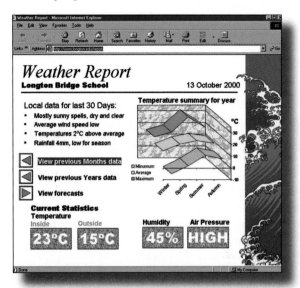

WHAT YOU HAVE TO DO

1. Decide on an audience that would benefit from your weather information e.g. sports, holiday, etc.

2. Collect electronic information on the local and/or national weather. This may include satellite pictures, raw data from weather stations, tables, graphs and charts. Look at a number of weather predictions for the next few days. Do they all agree? How different is any local forecast you find?

3. Prepare a presentation system suited to the audience you have targeted.

4. What access to information and communications technology will the audience need e.g. Internet access vs. printed material?

5. Decide on which information is required to communicate an appropriate amount of information to the audience (i.e. not too much and not too little detail).

6. How will you make it easy to understand? What presentation techniques will make the messages clearer?

IT at work

Here's how the Meteorological Office use ICT to produce the weather forecast you see on TV.

Automatic weather stations ■

'Every day the Meteorological Office produces forecasts for the weather that are carried in newspapers, radio and television. To make forecasts, a large number of observations have to be made and then the likely outcome predicted. Increasingly the process has become automated and computerised.

There are many observation sites around the country that collect the data we need to produce a forecast. These are run either by professional observers or volunteers. In the last twenty years **automatic weather stations (AWS)** have started to be used. New advances in technology have made these more accurate and cheaper to run.

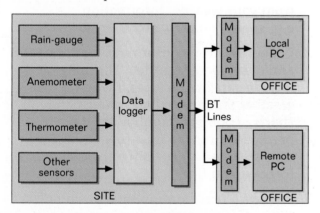

Automatic weather station schematic layout

A typical AWS normally consists of a set of weather sensors connected to a central data logger. This provides measurement, data processing and digital storage of sensor outputs. Loggers may run from mains power or battery and can transfer data by telephone or by continuous connection to a PC.

The station can collect most of the data needed to make forecasts such as air temperature, humidity, pressure, wind speed and direction, rainfall and sunshine.'

Achieving accuracy ■

'All of the instruments have to be carefully set and calibrated to ensure that they give accurate results. The AWS must also be positioned carefully because of the problem associated with buildings and wind turbulence.

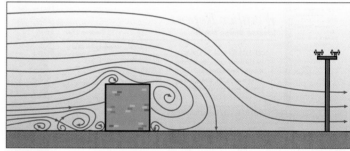

Wind flow around a building

Rainfall is surprisingly difficult to measure accurately because of air turbulence above the collecting funnel and the shadowing effect of nearby obstacles. Some elements traditionally obtained by visual observation are not easily measured by AWS. These include cloud amount and type, whether the ground is wet or dry, and measurement of snow depth.

All the measurements are transmitted to the Met. Office HQ. Here they use a **Cray Supercomputer** that runs a program or **model** to forecast the weather based on the available data.

The model is a program containing thousands and thousands of calculations. It is a model because it attempts to emulate the behaviour of the natural weather systems.'

Pictures by satellite ■

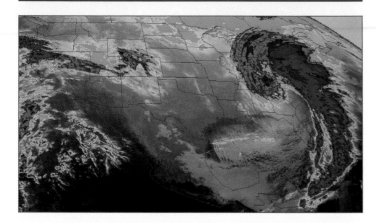

'The picture above is a UK Infra-Red Meteosat Image that comes in to the BBC Weather Centre from the Met. Office. They are updated at three hourly intervals. Unlike Visible Satellites, Infra-Red satellites measure the heat of particular objects (for example clouds or the surface of the sea).

The raw images are digitally encoded by the European Space Agency's Meteosat 7 satellite and beamed to an earth station in Germany, where they are processed. The Meteosat 7 Geostationary Satellite is located 36,000km above the planet's surface. It orbits around the Earth at the same speed as the Earth's spin. This means that it stays at the same point relative to the Earth's surface.'

Watching the weather on TV ■

'The very first television weather forecasts featured a presenter using a blackboard and a series of hand drawn charts. Today, the whole process is computerised.

Data in the form of a series of files that consist of forecast isobars, temperature contours, rainfall, and cloud cover arrives at the BBC Weather Centre twice a day. In addition they receive satellite images every three hours, and a whole range of other data. This whole process is automated and goes on day-in, day-out every day of the year.

The data goes straight to two DEC Alpha computers that directly interpret the data and produce the finished picture. It does this very quickly. For example, a satellite picture is ready in seven seconds! The TV weather broadcaster can have every chart ready for use at the touch of a button. Apple Macs provide the presenter with a user interface, but the display on their screens is now the finished image that will be used 'on air'.

There is a separate machine to replay the graphics in the studio, similar in concept to a video recorder but the storage is on computer hard disks.

This machine can process the next image as the first is being broadcast, so that the presenter can switch quickly between the images.

Of course these days you can also get the weather from the Web!'

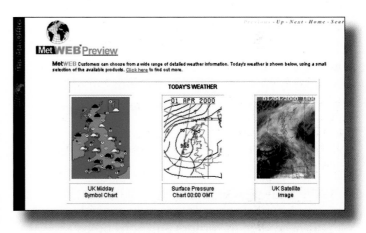

Weatherman and machine ■

'Despite greater computer power, improvements to the computer models, and other technological advances, there is still an important role for the forecaster. For the general development of weather systems, the model provides insight into how the atmosphere is behaving and developing, but it is only a guide. Good as it is, forecasters have to make allowances for the model's known problem areas. They also have to take into account any late observations and consult the latest satellite and radar pictures.

Without doubt, the combination of human forecaster and computer produces the best results.'

5 Control Systems

Computers are used to control many events that happen in our everyday lives. In this unit you will learn how to write programs that can control devices connected to a computer.

On Target

You should already know:

- how to write and correct simple Logo programs that create the effects that you want
- how to use automatic repetition and write your own customised commands
- how to use angles and geometry to achieve the effects that you want.

In this unit you will build on these skills and learn about:

- connecting a computer to the outside world
- using sensors to automatically control output devices such as motors and light bulbs
- designing and building systems that can automatically carry out a task.

Control systems can be modelled using a computer, some software and an interface box such as LEGO Dacta® or Smart box.

How is your life controlled? ■

Computers are not only the boxes that sit on your desk at school or home, they also have many other uses in everyday life. In your home you will find several devices that are controlled by computer processors. Just think about a typical day.

Your typical day?

- You are woken up by your radio alarm clock that automatically turns on the radio at 7.30 in the morning.
- You go into the kitchen and select a program on your microwave that will cook your breakfast.
- Before leaving for school you set your video recorder to tape your favourite programme because you are going to the cinema after school.
- On your way to school you stop at the local supermarket. As you walk up to the store the front doors open automatically.
- Inside you notice a person withdrawing cash from a cash dispenser.
- You choose a chocolate bar and hand it to the assistant who passes it under a barcode reader. The price and name of the product appears on the screen.
- After school you use your mobile phone to tell your parents what time to collect you.

All these electronic devices depend on control systems to make them work as you want them to.

Controlling interests

Computer control systems exist in many different forms. They may not necessarily involve what is normally thought of as a computer. For example, the computer may have no manual input, such as a keyboard. Some systems are totally manually controlled. All of these systems do, however, have one thing in common: they take an **input** and **process** it in some way to produce an **output**.

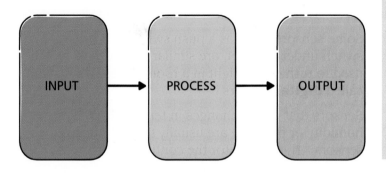

When you begin to design control systems it is vital that you are always clear about what should happen in each of these stages.

Task	Input	Process	Output
Turning on a light	Apply pressure to light switch	The electrical circuit is completed	The light bulb emits light
Turning on a tap	Rotate the top of the tap in an anti-clockwise direction	The valve inside the tap opens	Water flows into the sink
Unlocking a door	Insert the key into the lock and turn	If the key is the right shape the barrels allow the key to turn	The latch that is holding the door closed is released

This table shows how some simple control systems can be analysed in this way. Alternatively the inputs processes and outputs could be shown as a flow chart

Unlocking a door

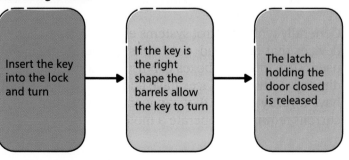

Getting IT Right in...

Design and Technology
A group of pupils were examining how cycling can reduce the environmental impact of travelling to work in large cities.

They decided to design a control technology system that would make the actual cycle journey safer. This involved a system of traffic lights that would give cyclists travelling along a cycle path right of way when they reached a road junction.

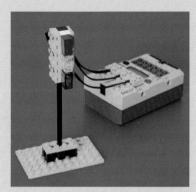

Complex systems

Many control systems involve more than just one input and one output, and may be required to carry out a range of tasks. For example, a system can be set up to automatically control the environment in a greenhouse. It will need to monitor the amount of light and water that all of the plants receive. It will also need to check the temperature constantly. If any of these fall outside the acceptable limits, the system would need to respond in a particular way.

For example, if there is a heatwave the moisture in the soil may evaporate very quickly. This would mean that more watering would be needed than normal. If the system only turned the sprinklers on once a week, the plants could be dead before they received any water. A solution would be to add moisture sensors to trigger the sprinklers as soon as the moisture levels fell too low.

WHAT YOU HAVE TO DO

1. **Make a list of some of the electronic control systems that operate in your school.**

2. **Imagine that you are going ten pin bowling. Write down all of the computer control systems that you might come across at the bowling alley.**

I. The interface

On this page you will learn how to connect input and output devices to your computer and use the computer to control the output devices.

Using an interface

In the last unit you looked at a physical interface that connected the computer to the outside world. This allowed you to attach sensors to the computer which then monitors and measures changes to the environment.

Here you will learn how to use the inputs from the sensors to control any outputs that are connected to the interface box. This will involve the use of a different type of interface that provides outputs as well as reading data from inputs.

The one shown here is produced by **LEGO**. The interface you have available might not be exactly the same one. Your teacher will explain what the differences are.

Inputs

In the last unit you looked at using **sensors** to measure the environment. When you build a control system you use sensors to tell your device what to do. It is important to use the right kind of sensor in order to make sure that your system will work properly. In some cases there may be more than one type of sensor that is suitable.

What sensor would you use in the following situations?

- A fire alarm system.
- A system that alerts you that your baby sister is crying.
- A system that automatically lights up your front garden when someone walks through the gate.

Some sensors, such as a push switch or a pressure switch under a carpet, are similar to an on/off switch used to turn on the light in a room. These are usually called **digital** sensors.

Sensors that detect changes in temperature, light, humidity or pressure are usually termed **analogue** sensors. These monitor the continuous changes that occur in the environment.

In control circuits it is usual to arrange that the system triggers a switch at a certain point. For example, 'when the temperature is greater than 30°C turn on the fan'.

Outputs

Through a suitable interface the computer can switch on and off almost any electrical device, even a mains lamp or a heater.

What output device would you expect to find in:

- a burglar alarm?
- a lift?
- an automatic door?

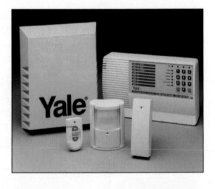

Generally when control systems are being modelled, devices that only need 6–12 volts to operate them are used. The interface boxes can usually control these directly. Some interfaces have additional outputs that have a **relay** system that can manage the larger current required to operate a motor.

Making the connection ■

Before you can build any type of control system it is important that you decide exactly what the system should do and think about how it should work. This will be covered later in this unit. However, before you can do this you need to understand how to connect your inputs and outputs and how to make them communicate with each other.

What you need

Make sure that the interface board is connected to the computer and that you have at least one input sensor and one output device chosen from the list below:

Inputs	Outputs
● a push switch	● a lamp
● a light sensor	● a motor
● a temperature sensor	● a buzzer

You will also need some connecting leads.

If you look at the interface board you will notice that there are a number of input connection points and a number of output points. Many interfaces have room for four inputs and four output devices. The LEGO system shown below has two types of inputs. Four are for inputs that require power and the other four are for the inputs that do not. There are also eight outputs.

If you have a LEGO system connect your input and output device in the same way as shown in the photograph below. If you are using a different control system you will need to consult your teacher.

The computer may need to be told what is actually attached to the interface board. However, many interface systems can automatically detect the inputs.

Monitoring the input ■

Make sure the LEGO Dacta software is loaded. Find the window that includes a picture of the top of the interface box.

● Click on the icon that represents one of your devices

● Hold down the left-hand mouse button then drag the icon on to the relevant port on the board

Your screen should look as like this:

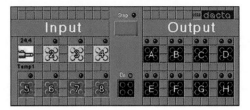

Above each icon that represents an input device you will see a number. This is the measurement that the sensor is sending to the computer. In the last unit you recorded this information and then presented your findings. Here you will learn how to use changes in these measurements to trigger output devices.

Change the environment of each sensor (e.g. shade the light sensor, or hold the temperature sensor between your fingers) to make sure that the system is working properly.

You can monitor input changes on screen by creating a graph from the Pages menu

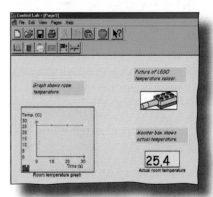

WHAT YOU HAVE TO DO

Write a short news report about a society in the future where everyday tasks are controlled completely by computers.

Explain what happened when the computers suddenly stopped working. How well could people remember how to carry out simple tasks?

2. Under control (I)

Some control systems work totally on their own, while others respond to changes in their environment. Here you will look at these different types of systems. First, however, you need to understand more about how control programs are written.

In command

To write a control program, the problem needs to be broken down into a series of small steps.. These series of steps are sometime called **procedures**.

Control systems can work in two different ways. **Open Loop** systems collect data from their immediate environment and use this to control the outputs. **Closed Loop** systems follow a series of pre-programmed actions.

Controlling the output devices ■

There are several ways that you can control your output devices. With the LEGO system the simplest is to use the mouse to click on one of the small green buttons above the relevant sensor. Try this with your output device.

● Is there any change when you click on the other button?

To turn devices on and off, control the output with a computer. LEGO uses a command centre where commands can be typed in, e.g.

        Talkto "motora

        On

This command should make the motor run continuously.

● What do you think you need to type to turn the motor off?

● How would you turn the light bulb on and then off?

If you are not using LEGO your control language will use a similar but unique set of commands to achieve the same result.

Writing a sequence of commands ■

By writing a simple program it is possible to group together a series of commands and run them in sequence. Look at the simple program on the right. Can you describe in words what actions you think it will make happen?

```
To Test1
Talkto "lampB
On Wait 50
Off
Talkto "motorA
On Wait 20
Off Wait 5
RD
On Wait 20
Off
Talkto "lampB
On Wait 50
Off
End
```

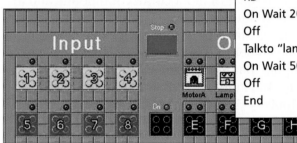

A simple control system used at supermarket entrances to open the doors when a customer approaches can be broken down as follows:

● Detect a person approaching the door. When a person approaches the door turn on the motors that control the doors.

● Stop the motors when the doors are fully open.

● Detect when the person has moved through the doors.

● Check to see that no one else is approaching the doors.

● Close the doors.

Breaking a problem down into smaller tasks makes it much easier to design a system that will work properly. This is because each individual part can be tested, and problems solved before putting the whole system together. These mini programs that carry out specific tasks are sometimes called **Procedures**.

 Inputs and outputs p90

Repeating a sequence ■

Once you have designed and tested the different procedures that you want to use in your program they will form the building blocks to create the final system.

An example of this is a system to control a set of four coloured lights at a school disco.

In designing the system you may have decided that you need three different events to happen:

- The lights flash one after the other in sequence.
- The lights all flash on and off at the same time.
- The lights flash randomly.

Once you have decided these simple events you will need to build up a complex program to make the light-show more interesting. You may decide to vary the length of time that the lights flash for and also vary the number of times that the sequence is carried out.

Linking inputs and outputs ■

Closed loop systems

The command procedure above is an example of a **closed loop system**. These tend to be used for the more simple types of control device. For example, a set of traffic lights that change colour every few minutes, regardless of whether or not cars are waiting at the junction.

When this type of device is manufactured a set of instructions will be programmed into the device. These instructions will either be carried out continuously or for the amount of time defined by the user.

If you want to cook something in your microwave for two minutes you set the time and then press the start button. The microwave will:

- turn on the motor that rotates the glass plate
- turn on the internal light
- start the cooking process
- wait for the time interval set before switching everything off, even if the food is ready sooner!

Open loop systems

More sophisticated control systems can be built that respond to changes in the environment rather than merely carrying out a set of instructions.

An **open loop** system will respond to the changes it has made to its environment as well as the initial input from the system. For example, a central heating system may be programmed to switch itself on at 5.30a.m. every day. Once the heating system is on it will monitor the temperature in the house and turn off the boiler when the temperature reaches the level set by the householder. If the temperature then falls below this level, the boiler will be turned back on again.

Most modern office blocks have something called an **environmental control system**. This type of system is used to keep the temperature of the building constant regardless of conditions outside. In order to do this the system includes both heating and cooling devices, as well as heat sensors.

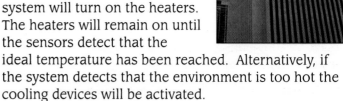

The sensors will send data to a central computer, which will compare the temperature with what has been set as the ideal. If the offices are too cold the system will turn on the heaters. The heaters will remain on until the sensors detect that the ideal temperature has been reached. Alternatively, if the system detects that the environment is too hot the cooling devices will be activated.

At all times the system is monitoring both the outside environment and also the effect that it has on the overall temperature.

On open loop system can be represented as a special type of diagram, known as a flow chart. You will learn more about these later in this unit.

WHAT YOU HAVE TO DO

Divide the list you made on page 89 of control systems in your school into those that are open loop and those that are closed loop.

3. Under control (2)

On this page you will learn how to build a simple control system that uses feedback.

Feedback

When a system monitors its own actions and uses this data to decide on further actions it is said to be using **feedback**. This is very important in developing systems that work automatically, independent of human intervention.

Feedback has a very long history. The Romans were famed for their engineering feats, one of which was the building of aqueducts. The water level in these was controlled by a simple floating valve, that opened when more water was needed and closed when the appropriate level was reached.

Getting the temperature of the water right when you take a shower is a more familiar example. You feel the water, turn the control to make it hotter or colder, feel the water again, turn the tap again, and so on until the water is exactly the right temperature.

Can you think of any other feedback systems in your home?

For a computer-based system to use feedback it is important that any data is converted into a signal that the computer can understand. In the previous unit you explored how to use sensors to monitor and measure the environment. You were introduced to analogue and digital signals. The data that you used to draw graphs and present as tables is the same data that a control system will use as feedback.

For example, the heating system in your home may include a thermostat that allows you to control the temperature. The system will measure the temperature of the house and if it is below the required temperature it will turn on the boiler. The temperature is constantly monitored until it reaches the required level. At this point the boiler will be turned off until the temperature falls.

Keeping the burglars away

You are now going to design and make a system that could be used to fool burglars into thinking that you are at home when you are in fact away. You are going to build a system that automatically turns on a light when it gets dark.

You will be using a **Light Dependant Resistor (LDR)** to measure the light level. You will need to tell the program how dark it needs to be before the light is to come on.

The system

You will need to connect the LDR to one of the inputs on the interface box, and a lamp to an output. If you are using LEGO make sure that you use exactly the same connections as shown in the photograph.

You will need to tell the computer what you have connected to the interface box.

- Left click on the lamp icon and drag it to output A
- Left click on the light icon and drag it to input 5

Your screen should look like the one below.

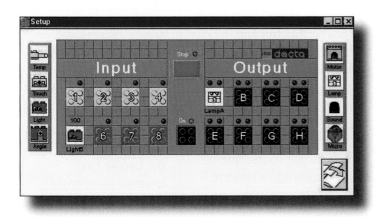

In control

You now need to write the program that will control your system.

You need to tell the computer to turn on **light A** when it becomes dark. You will need to translate *dark* into something that the computer will understand. To do this you need to decide the light level that you will call *dark*. Remember most people turn on their lights when it is beginning to get dark and do not wait until it is completely black outside.

You can type the code below into the procedures page. You will need to set the light level that works best in your situation. The procedure is called **burstop**.

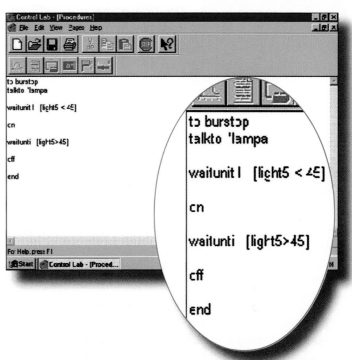

```
to burstop
talkto 'lampa

waitunitl [light5 < 37]

on

waitunti [light5>45]

off

end
```

The procedure that you have just written includes more instructions than just turning on the light. For this system to work effectively the light needs to be turned off when it becomes daylight again.

Make sure that you understand which part of the procedure turns on the lamp and which part turns it off.

To test the program, switch to the command centre and type:

- **burstop**

You should now be able to turn the light on by shading the light sensor. You may need to adjust the light level settings to make the system work properly.

WHAT YOU HAVE TO DO

Write down clear instructions explaining how to set up your burglar deterrent system. These instructions will be used by pupils who have not used the LEGO system before.

4. Planning a simple system

On this page you will see how important it is to plan a system properly before you try to build it.

Planning matters

You are about to design and build your own control system. Here you will learn that it is very important that you plan exactly what you want your system to do before you build it. You also need to work out exactly how you are going to test your system.

It is important that any system is tested in all situations before other people are allowed to use it. If not you could end up with a system that does not work or, more importantly, one that is dangerous.

The **hardware** and **software** in control systems need to be considered individually and also designed to work together.

The problem

You are going to plan a control system that will automatically control a car park barrier. The barrier will raise when a car approaches it and then fall after the car has passed. The first thing that you need to do is to break down the problem into separate stages. There are many ways of doing this but the simplest is probably a list.

It is very important that you include all of the required actions in your list. What would happen if you forgot to include the command to reverse the direction of the motor?

Car drives up to barrier

Sensor detects car

Barrier motor turned on

Sensor detects that the barrier is raised high enough

Motor turned off

Sensor detects car has passed the barrier

Motor direction is reversed

Motor turned on

Sensor detects that the barrier has lowered sufficiently

Motor turns off

Wait for next car

What will the barrier look like?

You now need to think about how you can build a model that will represent the car park barrier. It would be very expensive and time consuming to build a full size barrier! For this project you are going to use a construction kit. The photograph on the left is of a suitable model using LEGO. Look very closely at the photograph to help you think about a suitable design that will include all of the features needed to test if your idea will actually work.

Inputs

You need to think about what sensors to use. The system needs to sense automatically when a car drives up to the barrier. There are two possible ways that you could achieve this with LEGO Dacta. You could use either the **light** or the **touch/contact** sensor.

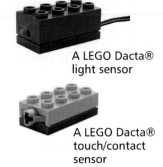

A LEGO Dacta® light sensor

A LEGO Dacta® touch/contact sensor

● Draw a diagram of where you think each could be incorporated into the system.

The system also needs to detect the position of the barrier arm. To do this you need to use the **angle** sensor. The picture on the left shows how this is incorporated into the design.

Testing as you go

When you carry out any type of problem solving activity you will at some point need to discover if your solution actually works.

You could build your model, write the program, turn everything on and find the system works perfectly. Unfortunately this is very unlikely! Probably if you waited until you had completed everything, nothing would happen when you first turned the system on. You would then have the problem of finding out exactly what is causing the problem or problems. You would not be sure if the problem was with your model or with the program. Even if you were fairly sure it was something to do with the program you would still have to search through all of your work for what could turn out to be a simple typing error.

A much better way of working is to test your design in small chunks. For example, when you are building the barrier model connect the motor to a suitable power supply and check that the mechanism works. Check that the model is robust by operating it several times.

When you are writing your program check each procedure before adding it to your final program.

Software

As well as designing a physical device you will need to write a computer program that will actually control the device. On the last page you wrote a simple program called a **procedure** to control a light being turned on and off. When you are sure that your design works manually you can start to plan how your control program will work.

Designing the program

When you are happy with the design of your barrier you need to think about the program to control it. Below is a LEGO procedure for detecting the car as it arrives at the barrier and raising the barrier to a set position.

● Describe in your own words what you think each line of this procedure does.

```
To enter
Talkto "motora
Waituntil [entry > 50]
On
Waituntil [armangle > 85]
Off
End
```

To complete the control system the program needs to monitor constantly the value of the entry sensor. It also has to lower the barrier after the car has driven through it. The whole command sequence will have a number of sections responding to the input and the output it is controlling.

WHAT YOU HAVE TO DO

1. **Build a model of the barrier using a kit or components such as motors, gears, pulleys and sensors you have available.**

2. **Check the outputs work by manually operating the control circuit or using a command in the software.**

3. **Discuss how realistic the model is. What are its limitations?**

5. Go with the flow

Here you will learn how to draw a special type of diagram called a flow chart. This will allow you to present a control process in a graphical form. This makes it easier to check.

Flow charts

A flow chart helps you to describe the flow of information through a system. All of the separate actions involved in a control process are represented. This allows you to check the flow of data and actions.

The symbols to use

There are some simple symbols used to construct a flow chart.

The **start/stop** box is used to show the beginning and end of a sequence of commands.

The **input/output** box is used to represent actions that either the system responds to, or that cause the system to respond. In the example of running a bath, actions such as 'putting in the plug' and 'turning on the tap' are represented inside this symbol.

The **process** box is used to represent something that the system does, either in response to an input or to cause an output. It is the part that actually controls what is going on.

The **decision box** is a very important symbol. It is used to represent the 'thinking parts' of your program. It is also a very useful planning tool, because it makes you break down the problem into logical steps. You use this type of symbol to ask questions about what actions your inputs or outputs will cause.

The first decision box in the 'running a bath' flow chart asks 'Is the water too hot?'. Without this check you could end up with a bath that is filled to the correct level, but could be far too hot to get into. Similarly, the next decision is there to make sure that the bath is not too cold. It is important that these checks are carried our regularly until the desired result is achieved.

Drawing a flow chart

Using these symbols you can develop a picture that represents most processes. For example you can represent running a bath in the following way.

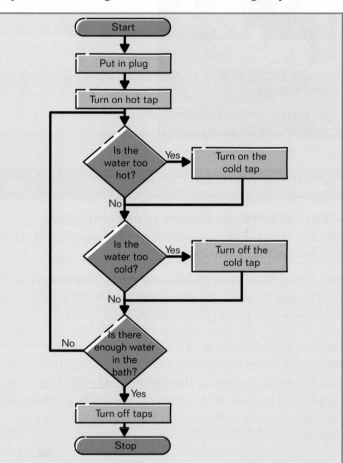

In this example, the answer 'no' to the question 'is there enough water in the bath?' returns the flow back to the question about the water being too hot.

- Can you see the decision loops? Where does the feedback come from to make the decision?
- In this case who is receiving the feedback?
- How is the system being controlled?

AutoShapes

To help you draw your own flow charts you can use the drawing program that is part of Microsoft *Word*. This has a floating menu bar called **AutoShapes**. One set of Autoshapes are the symbols you need to draw a flow chart.

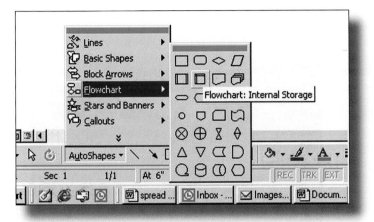

Drawing the barrier system

You are now going to develop a flow chart for the car park barrier system that you examined in the last unit. We will start with the **input** section.

The system constantly monitors the sensor. Only when it detects a car does something happen.

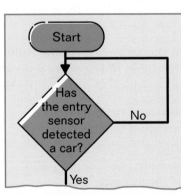

The car can now safely enter the car park. The next thing that we need to do is make sure that the car is past the barrier before the system lowers the barrier again.

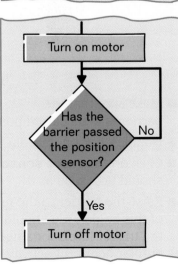

Finally the motor needs to be switched off when the barrier has returned to a horizontal position. The system then needs to be told to go back to monitoring the entry sensor.

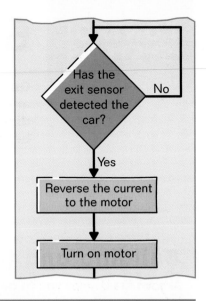

Control from flow charts

Some pieces of software allow you to draw a flow chart on the screen. This is automatically converted to a control program. Even without this type of software it is good design practice to use the flow chart as a way of planning a control program.

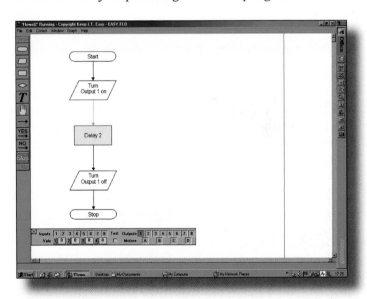

WHAT YOU HAVE TO DO

1. **Put the three elements of the system together to form a complete flow chart that represents the car park barrier system.**

2. **Extend the flow chart to show how the system could sense if it was safe to lower the barrier.**

6. It really works!

On this page you will learn how to turn your flow chart and model into a working system. Things can go disastrously wrong if a system is not properly tested before being used, and also regularly when in use.

Aeroplanes are systematically and thoroughly checked before every flight. Even a minor problem can lead to catastrophic failure

Building and testing the system

You should now have a model of the car park barrier, and a flow chart of how you think the system should work. On this page you will write the program code that you will use to control your system, connect everything to the computer and finally test it to see if it works!

Putting it all together ■

Before you can write your program you need to establish the data range of your sensors. Make sure that the interface box is connected to your computer and that your sensors are correctly connected. If you are using the LEGO control system they should be as follows:

Entry light sensor	Input 5
Exit light sensor	Input 6
Angle sensor	Input 7
Motor	Output A

Next you need to tell the computer what is attached to the interface box. If you are using the LEGO Dacta **Control Lab** setup screen it should look like this:

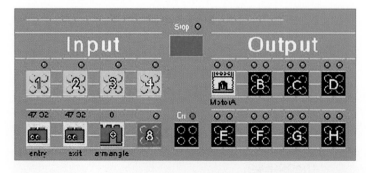

To make your program easier to understand it is a good idea to change the names of the sensors to something that is more useful. To do this double-click on the icon and then type in the new name in the appropriate slot.

In the sequence on the right **entry** has been used as the name of the entry light sensor and **arm angle** for the position sensor on the barrier.

Next you need to work out what will be your trigger readings to activate the various parts of the system.

Click here

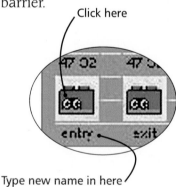

Type new name in here

- Make sure that the barrier is in its closed position
- Double-click on its icon
- Click on the **reset sensor** button. The angle should now read as 0
- Raise the barrier to the required level. Make a note of this angle. You should have already measured the trigger levels for a light sensor in the earlier burglar deterrent activity

Programming

You have already been introduced to procedures. You are now going to write a series of procedures which you will then put together to create your control program. If you are using the LEGO Dacta **Control Lab**:

● Choose the **procedures** screen from the **Pages** menu

With the LEGO system you can type a series of procedures. The software will recognise the end of one and go to the beginning of the next.

● Type the following commands:

```
To enter
Talkto "motora
Waituntil [entry > 50]
On
Waituntil [armangle > 85]
Off
End

To close
Talkto"motora
Waituntil [exit > 50]
Rd
On
Waituntil [armangle =0]
Off
End

To barrier
Repeat
Enter
Close
End
```

● Return to the command centre and type 'barrier'. Your system should now be active and you can test it to see if it works.

Testing

The first thing that you need to do is check that the system works in normal conditions. You also need to think about the entire range of conditions in which your control system is likely to be used.

You need to write down all of the possible situations. For example:

● What happens when it gets dark?

● What happens if two or more cars are in the system at the same time?

● What happens if a person walks by the sensor?

You will probably find that your system does not pass all of these tests!

If the systems that control a nuclear reactor are not reliable and regularly checked, the results can be devastating

Controlling the flow of traffic is a difficult task. An unexpected problem in one place can quickly cause extensive delays over a wide area.

WHAT YOU HAVE TO DO

1. **Describe how you could improve the system to avoid some of the faults that occurred when testing was carried out.**

2. **Make notes to show how you would redesign the system to make it function properly.**

7. Ins and Outs

On this page you will learn that a computer can respond to multiple sensors to control one or more devices at the same time.

What are the options?

Next you will learn that a computer control system can be made up of many **inputs** that in turn control a range of **outputs**.

To help you understand how these systems are designed and work you are going to analyse some more complex systems and then draw the flow chart that explains how they work. If necessary, revise the work that you did on flow charts and make sure that you are familiar with how to include a decision in your diagram.

In sequence

Computer based control systems can process a number of inputs and then control a variety of outputs depending on the data that they receive.

The example systems that you have built so far have all been **sequential**. This means that one action has followed (or has been caused) by another. This is how many control systems do actually work in the real world. It is useful however to be able to build systems that do not work in this sequential way.

It may be important that a system makes a decision based on the signal that it receives from a number of sensors. A good example of this is the security system installed in a large modern building. If the system was sequential then it would wait for a response from the *first* sensor listed in the program rather than responding to *any* sensor.

Security system

In the security system of a large building the activation of the alarm needs to be triggered by whichever sensor is activated. It is also important that this system indicates where the intrusion has taken place so that the security guards can check what has happened as quickly as possible.

Avoiding triggering a sensor can be a Mission Impossible!

Car park barrier system

A real car park barrier system uses many inputs to trigger one output.

The car park barrier system that you created was a very simple system that just raised the barrier when a car approached and closed the barrier when the car was safely past. In reality there would need to be more decisions made by the system. In fact the decision to open the barrier would be dependent on a number of inputs.

The next section describes the different **states** the system needs to be in to work properly.

i   Inputs and outputs *p90*

The state of the system

The relationship between the parts of the system can be represented in something called a **state table**. This takes all of the sequence of inputs and depending on what they are sensing, states the various components of the system.

Below is the car park entry barrier system presented as a state table. It assumes that the barrier will only lift if there is a space in the car park and the car driver has taken a ticket.

Sequence of events	System components				
	Light/ pressure sensor before gate	Counter below maximum?	Ticket sensor	Light/ pressure sensor after barrier	Barrier motor
No car	nil	yes	nil	nil	off
Car drives up	yes	yes	nil	nil	off
Driver takes ticket	yes	yes	yes	nil	on
Car drives through barrier	nil	yes	nil	yes	stop reverse on stop
		1 added to counter			
No car	nil	yes	nil	nil	off

- Draw a state table for the exit of the car park
- Use both of these state tables to draw a flowchart of the whole system

A greenhouse for the future

A greenhouse for the future uses many inputs and many outputs working simultaneously. Commercial greenhouses are used to grow vegetables over an extended period of the year by providing them with a controlled environment. They provide a more sheltered environment than a garden, but they can also cause problems.

In the winter they can be very cold while in the heat of the summer they can be quite the opposite. Because the roof prevents the plants being watered naturally there needs to be some method of watering them.

A design for a system that automatically controls the conditions in the greenhouse would have to use a variety of sensors and different output devices. This can be summarised as:

Problem	Sensor	Output device(s)
too cold in winter	temperature	heater
too hot in summer	temperature	fan or blinds over the windows
plants need watering	moisture	watering system

The flow chart for this system has much in common with the flow chart on page 98 which describes the process of filling a bath to the right temperature. The greenhouse system is, however, automated and includes many more inputs and outputs.

- Draw the flow chart for this system

A more sophisticated version of this system is used in the tropical greenhouses in Kew Gardens, where the plants need to be fooled into thinking that they are in the tropics, rather than south west London.

WHAT YOU HAVE TO DO

Write a list of all the control systems you can think of that use either multiple inputs or outputs.

8. Another brick in the wall

Finally in this unit you will design and build a complex control system.

Designing complex systems

You have now been introduced to the basics of designing and building control systems. You have been taken through the various planning stages and should also be aware of the need to test your system carefully. You are now going to work as part of a team that will design and build a factory distribution system.

There are four components to this system:

- The conveyor belt
- The ram
- The yellow block buggy
- The blue block buggy.

Your teacher will provide you with exact designs for these items.

I, Robot

Modern factories use computers and robots in many different ways. They are used to assemble parts, to paint the final products, and also to keep track of the progress of all of the items that are in production at any point in time. For this activity you are going to look at the distribution of the final products.

The delivery problem

A factory manufactures yellow and blue LEGO blocks. After the production process both colours are fed onto a conveyor belt. The yellow blocks need to be able to travel to the end of the conveyor belt where they will be collected and put into a buggy that will deliver them to their storage point.

There are fewer blue blocks. When one passes a sensor the conveyor belt should stop and a ram should push the blue brick off the conveyor down a slide where it is loaded onto a separate buggy that then delivers the brick to a different area of the factory. The system should stop and wait if either buggy is not in its proper place to receive the bricks.

Stand alone robots

If you are using the LEGO system you will need the RCX unit. This can be programmed by infra-red directly from your computer.

Many modern control systems allow you to build separate parts of the system that do not have to be physically connected to the computer. With some systems you write the control program by using the associated software and then download the instructions to a small on-board computer that is built into your model. One example of this is the Programmable Chips (PICs) system.

LEGO **Robolab** is another example. It uses the same sensors and output devices that you are are used to working with. The main difference is that it uses a

Drawing a flow chart *p98* The state of a system *p103*

graphics-based, rather than a text-based system of programming. A simple program is shown below. Can you work out what this program does?

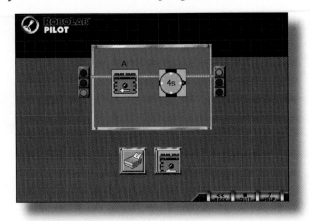

How does it all fit together?

Before you can create a flow chart of your particular aspect of the project you need to think about how all of the parts fit together. In order to do this you can produce a state table. The table below has been partially completed. Discuss this in your group and complete the blanks.

Sequence of events	System components					
	Conveyor belt	Brick colour sensor	Grabber mouth motor	Grabber rotation sensors	Line following sensor	Destin- ation

Flow charts

Once you have agreed how the various parts fit together and trigger the various responses you now need to create a flow chart of the control system for your particular part of the project.

On Target

You should now be able to:

- connect a computer to the outside world
- use sensors to control output devices such as motors and light bulbs automatically
- design and build systems that can automatically carry out a task.

Writing the programs

There is an old saying that there is no point re-inventing the wheel. This means that it is a waste of time to do something that has already been done by somebody else.

When you produce graphics on your computer you quite often use a clip art library that includes lots of ready-made drawings. The same is true of control programming. For example, the LEGO Robolab software is supplied with a range of pre-written routines and programs. Within the **Amusement Park** theme there is a program called **Tour Bus 2.vi**. This uses a light sensor that detects the difference between light and dark to control the motors of a buggy. The buggy has been designed to follow a black line.

This should give you a clue for the main control routines for your program. The buggies could follow a pre-drawn black line, and the selection of the bricks is dependent on the system sensing colour.

Testing the system

When you build a complex system that involves several inputs and outputs that control a range of devices it is important to be systematic in your testing. If you tried to test the whole thing at once you could end up with a terrible mess.

You must make sure that each component responds correctly to a manual input and processes it properly and then provides the correct input for the next link in the system.

You then need to check that all the safeguards are in place. For example, the conveyor belt should stop if the yellow buggy is not in position and the ram should leave the blue brick until the blue buggy returns.

WHAT YOU HAVE TO DO

1. **Write a user manual for your component of the system. You should include details of how the system works, and an explanation of your program in case any future users wish to change it in any way.**

2. **Draw a flow chart that incorporates all of the aspects of the system.**

IT at work

Philip Rodrigo is Production Unit Manager at Avesta Sheffield. Here he explains how computer systems are used to ensure that the company is producing the highest quality steel for the lowest possible costs.

Avesta Sheffield is one of Europe's largest manufacturers and distributors of stainless steel. The company has its operations in the UK, Sweden and the USA and sales offices around the world.

The UK operations are based in Sheffield. Over the last 50 years, the number of stainless steel companies in Sheffield and the number of people working in the industry has decreased significantly. Avesta Sheffield is the only large-scale manufacturer left in the city, however the company produces more stainless steel than all of the steel plants from 50 years ago used to make.

Avesta Sheffield needs to compete in an international market and therefore needs to be able to supply high quality stainless steel at the best possible prices. To achieve this, the company relies on the skill of its employees and the use of technology.

The use of computer systems in Avesta Sheffield is key to the operation of the company. The logging of customer orders is typically the first part of the business process where computers are used. Customer orders can be placed via the Internet or through conventional sales offices. If the required material can be supplied from existing stock then it is.

When the customer wants a special grade of steel or doesn't want the material immediately then their requirements will be matched with similar requirements from other customers and produced from scratch.

In production

At the start of the production process in Sheffield, Avesta Sheffield melts stainless steel scrap and ferro-alloys in an electrical arc furnace. The company buys nearly all of the stainless steel scrap generated in the UK as well as buying scrap and alloys from overseas.

A computer system is used to track all the stocks of material in the scrapyard in Sheffield and ensures that the appropriate reordering of raw materials is flagged-up to the relevant buyers.

The system is also used to generate the lowest scrap cost mix to create a customer requirement from the available material in the scrapyard.

Once melted, the liquid steel goes through a steel refining process where the chemical composition of the steel in brought in line with what the customer has ordered. When the steel has reached the correct chemical composition, it is then cast and cut into slabs weighing up to 28 tonnes and measuring 11 metres in length.

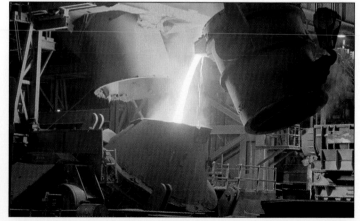

Slabs are then sent away from the site for an intermediate hot rolling process and then returned to the Sheffield site to be rolled into large coils of stainless steel of different thicknesses and widths.

The large coils are then cut up into smaller pieces to meet the requirements of the individual customers. These smaller pieces will be stainless steel sheets or coils which are then stored in a large distribution centre equipped with an automatic storage and retrieval system.

Automatic Storage and Retrieval

When a customer order is completed, the material is packed and then sent to the warehouse. The Automatic Storage and Retrieval (AS&R) system then stores the pack in one of 15,000 locations in an unmanned store. A transport system then groups together any packs that are to be sent to customers that are close to each other and a lorry is ordered and instruction given on what packs to collect.

This process is fully automated. When the lorry arrives on site, the driver hands in the list of packs for collection and the AS&R system picks out the packs and moves them to the lorry collection point. During times when lorries are not being loaded, the AS&R system automatically moves packs around the warehouse to ensure that those packs that are due for collection are moved to racks closer to the despatch point. This ensures that time is minimised when the lorry arrives to pick up the packs.

Customer requirements for stainless steel may range from architectural cladding to industrial piping and from transport tankers to surgical equipment.

Process control

At the **management information** level, the computer systems are used to schedule material designated for customers through the production process whilst minimising stock. These systems are used to provide the operators with information to allow them to make decisions.

At the **process control** level, computers are used to control various items of plant and machinery to ensure that the various systems such as sales order handling, production operations and despatching, communicate with each other.

In the **office environment**, the use of computers means that the administrative burden on logistics, finance and purchasing is minimised.

Over recent years the use of Windows-based applications, the Internet and laptops has improved the productivity and capability of the office-based employees. The issues with IT in a company like Avesta Sheffield relate to:

● keeping up with technology as the pace of change is very fast
● ensuring that employees are trained in how to use and exploit some of the IT products available
● making sure that the company has access to good IT people to support and develop the systems.

The use of computers is an integral part of producing and selling stainless steel. Increased productivity and cost savings have been generated through the use of IT putting Avesta Sheffield in a position to compete on an international stage.

6 Spreadsheets and Databases

In this unit you will follow three pupils as they use a spreadsheet and database to set up a system for a video shop.

On Target

You should already know:

- how data is stored in a structured form
- how a data table is organised using **fields**
- how to create forms using the **Form Wizard**.

In this unit you will learn how to use databases, spreadsheets and word processing to:

- edit and change database form layouts
- use **Queries** to interrogate your database
- use **Mail Merge** in word processing
- use multiple sheets and **Absolute Cell Referencing** in spreadsheets.

The programs used are **Microsoft Excel** and *Access*. If you have different packages you will find they contain very similar tools and functions, though they might be located in different places.

Databases and spreadsheets have found their way into the very core of Information Technology processes for industry and business. They are now essential tools for everybody to be able to do their work efficiently.

A busy customer call centre

Databases

In its simplest form a database stores data in an organised way. A database does not have to be an electronic one – a card file index is a database. However, an electronic database has a major advantage over a paper-based one – the data can be sorted in dozens of different ways.

Asking the right questions

All databases need data. The data collection is perhaps the most important part of the database.

Market researchers collect a great deal of information about what we do and our likes and dislikes. This data has to be input into a computer. It can take a long time to enter the results of thousands of questionnaires.

To make this job easier and quicker it is important to design the database and the questionnaire together. The answers to the questions need to be recorded in a way that will be as easy as possible to enter into the database. The database needs to be set up to make it as easy as possible to enter the answers.

Spreadsheets p120 IT at work p128 Using skills with spreadsheets and databases p138, p1

Preparing a questionnaire

Make sure you know exactly what information is required. Then think of some questions that are going to provide that information.

- Yes/No questions are the easiest to record and input. All you need to do is put a tick in the box for 'yes' or a cross for 'no'.

- You may want to ask people for a response on a scale of 1 to 5. Again this produces a number which is easy to enter into the database.

- The type of question to avoid is what is called an 'open-ended' question. For example, 'What is your opinion of....?'

Meanwhile, the visual appearance of the database entry screen needs to be considered. Remember that the information from the questionnaire should mirror the database screen wherever possible. Setting it out in a clear, logical series of steps helps a lot. At the same time making it look colourful and attractive will help keep the operator going.

What are your favourite sort of chips?

Spreadsheets ▪

Businesses use spreadsheets to record their accounts. The important thing to remember here is that business accounting does not change from month to month or year to year.

If a company sets up a spreadsheet to monitor its accounts in January then the same format can be used for February. The whole year can then be copied into the spreadsheet with minimal effort.

Spreadsheets are good at this. They have standard formats but different data. Formulas in the spreadsheet work on any data in the cells and they automatically work out the calculations. The result is minimal work and accurate results.

Getting IT Right in...

Business Studies

A business class investigated why the school tuck shop takings were falling. They designed a questionnaire and recorded the results in a spreadsheet for several months.

They recorded:

- the age range of pupils buying food
- the best selling brands of sweets
- the worst selling brands of sweets
- the profit margins on the sweets sold.

Creating a spreadsheet and charting the results helped the pupils by:

- analysing the relationship between the profit margin of sweets sold and the best selling sweets.

- comparing the types of sweets sold to the age range of the pupils.

The results of the analysis restored the tuck shop to profitability.

WHAT YOU HAVE TO DO

1. **Ask your parent/guardian for their junk mail or look through magazines for the free leaflets.**

2. **Make a study of the forms that the companies want you to fill in for credit cards and CD clubs.**

   - **Look at what type of information they want.**

   - **Think about the fields on the database where the information written down will end up. What fields will be needed?**

I. Shuffling the cards

On this page you will see how a database was used to help organise a video shop.

Video shop

Zoë, Kate and James worked with spreadsheets and databases to help Zoë's mother run her video shop more efficiently.

The problem with the video shop was that everything was written out by hand and all the financial work was done using calculators. This was very time consuming, so Zoë and her friends looked at ways to cut down on the amount of time that the current manual system used.

They used a database to develop a system for recording customer details and monitoring their video rentals. **Mail Merge** made sending reminders a great deal easier.

Spreadsheets helped to record financial data. This was then used to identify and analyse the areas of the business that could make Zoë's mother the most profit.

In this unit you can follow Zoë, Kate and James' thoughts and ideas as they set about solving the problem. You will see how they:

- designed tables
- chose fields
- investigated field properties.

The software packages used as examples in this unit are **Microsoft Excel** and **Microsoft Access**. The packages that you use in school might not be exactly the same, but you will still be able to do the work.

The project

To begin with, Zoë and her friends needed to analyse the system being used at present in the video shop.

They discovered that Zoë's mother was using a paper card system to keep track of the videos rented out. She also wrote orders out by hand. The system worked reasonably well, but business was getting better and she was starting to find that there was not enough time in the day for her to do everything properly. She also found that her card file index was getting so big that customers were having to wait a long time while she found their details.

Meanwhile, an increasing number of videos were not being returned on time, and sales were being lost. A quicker way was needed to get a letter sent out to the borrower.

Zoë also wanted to find out what would happen if the number of staff was reduced, or a different video supplier was used.

Card system ∎

The first thing the pupils did was to look at the card system. They soon realised that the card system was in fact a **database** – it was like an address book with slightly more information in it.

Membership number: _____

Name: _____

Address: _____

_____

Post Code: _____

Date joined: __/__/__

Creating tables ∎

The pupils set about using the information on the cards to create some tables in the database.

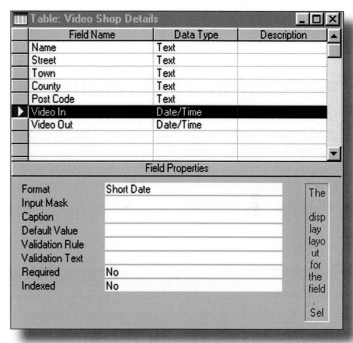

To create the table you see above, James entered **Field Names** and gave each of them a **Data Type**.

● What have they done to the address? Why do you think that they have done this?

● Is the **Field Size** of 50 characters long suitable for a name? What do you think that it should be? (You could investigate the length of people's names in your class.)

Data Types ∎

Zoë entered the **Data Types**. There are two shown on the database. Each data type has a **Format**. The format for the 'Video In' field is a **Short Date** – e.g. 29/09/99.

● Why do you think that they have used this format rather than use a format like 29 September 1999?

Completing the task ∎

On the next page you will see how the pupils investigated the design of their table further. They put in an **Input Mask** for the Post Code to make **data entry** easier.

WHAT YOU HAVE TO DO

1. **Create a table that can be used for entering the customer details.**

2. **You can use the field names shown on this page as a starting point. Add any others that you think may be required.**

3. **Select suitable Field Properties and data type formats for each of your chosen fields.**

2. On form

Here you will see how Zoë designed a screen to input and view data.

Working more formally

Up to now you have probably used **Form Wizards** to construct forms from your tables. The Wizards create good-looking forms but these are not always what are required. Sometimes you may need different layouts so that the user can easily see where to enter data.

Grouping

To begin with, Zoë used the **Form Wizard** to create a form.

However, she decided that she was not happy with the form that the Wizard had created. She wanted to change the way the data was grouped to make it easier for her mother to view it.

Zoë clicked on the **Design View** icon on the tool bar. Design View is used to change the appearance of a form.

The fields appear like drawings in a graphic package. Just like normal graphics they can be sized and moved using the mouse.

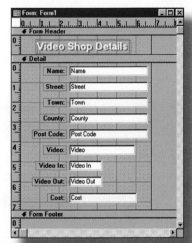

She used the pointer to click on the fields.

Black 'grab handles' appeared around the selected field.

When the pointer is moved over the selected field the pointer changes to a black hand. When the hand appears the fields can be moved.

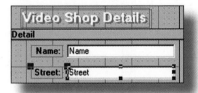

Re-designing the form

Here's how Zoë re-designed the form. She decided that there were three distinct groups:

- The name and address
- The video rental dates
- The video title and rental cost.

Zoë moved the pointer over the fields she wanted to move and clicked on them. She then dragged and dropped the field to a new location on the form.

Next, Zoë drew some lines using the line option on the **toolbox** to divide up her form.

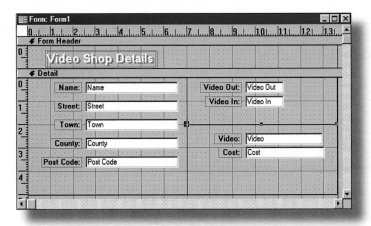

Zoë was still not happy with the way the form looked and decided to change the grey appearance to something a bit more eye-catching.

Colouring in

In **Design View** Zoë used the **palette** icon on the tool bar to bring up the palette. She used this to alter the colours of the revised form.

The **Fore Color** is the colour of the text in the field.
The **Back Color** changes the colour of the field.

Using the Toolbox

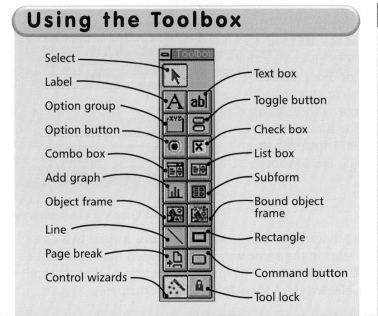

By using the mouse and selecting the fields to change, Zoë created a completely different looking form. Remember that to change anything you must have the black 'grab handles' around the field.

See what happens:

● if you hold the **Shift** key down and click on more than one field

● when you move the field using the black hand as a pointer. (Hint: try using the top left 'Grab Handle').

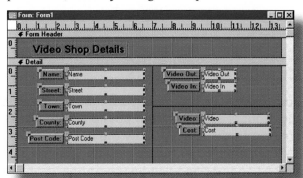

Compare the layout below with the original one created by the Wizard.

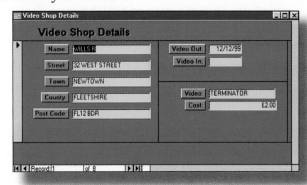

WHAT YOU HAVE TO DO

1. **Use the Form Wizard to create your own form.**

2. **Use Design View to edit the form.**

   ■ **Create a new layout.**

   ■ **Use different colours and lines to improve the overall look of your form.**

   ■ **Compare the edited form with the one you originally created and explain why the new layout is better than the old one.**

3. **Experiment further with the toolbox and palette to see what else you can change and design.**

3. The Mask

On this page you will continue looking at other useful ways to construct your database.

Accurate access

Zoë and Kate want to make sure that the data being input is as accurate as possible. One easy way to do this is to only allow the right type of data to be entered in the first place. There are two ways that **Access** can help with this problem:

- **Input Masks**: this tool lets you select some common formats for entering data.

- **Validation**: this is a way of making sure that a user enters data in the right format and spells it correctly.

Here you will see how Zoë and Kate used these two features.

Input Masks

It is important that the data input into the database is as accurate as possible. The **Input Mask** will ensure that data is entered in the correct format. What the input mask does is to provide imaginary boxes for data to go in.

The input mask will only allow the correct number of characters in the right format to be entered. You will not be allowed to put a square peg in a round hole…it just will not fit!

For example, a date must be written like this: 23/12/00. The input mask would be 99/99/99. Only numbers are allowed, up to a maximum of six. If you try and enter text, or more than 6 numbers, **Access** will tell you that you have made a mistake.

- Why is this type of input mask still prone to errors? Can you think what those errors are?

- Why is it important that data input is accurate?

- What may happen in the video shop if the data is not accurate?

To use input masks, Kate clicked on the icon in **Table Design** view. Then she used the Wizard displayed to select the mask she wished to use.

Kate made sure it was what she wanted and clicked **Finish**.

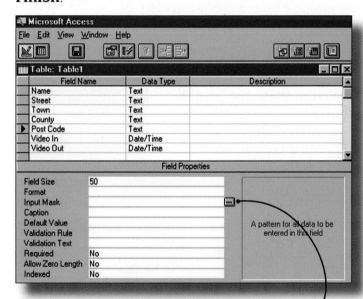

In Table Design View, click here to open the Input Mask Wizard

Kate used the **Input Mask Wizard** to help make sure that the **Post Codes** were entered correctly. She used the mouse to click on **Input Mask** in the Field Properties.

Use the **Try it** at the bottom to check that the Post Code will enter correctly

Kate used the **Input Mask Wizard** for the two date fields in the same way. She repeated the steps as for the Post Code. This time she made sure that she had selected the **Video In** or **Video Out** fields.

Validation

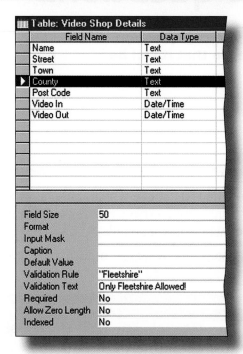

Table: Video Shop Details

Field Name	Data Type
Name	Text
Street	Text
Town	Text
County	Text
Post Code	Text
Video In	Date/Time
Video Out	Date/Time

Field Size	50
Format	
Input Mask	
Caption	
Default Value	
Validation Rule	"Fleetshire"
Validation Text	Only Fleetshire Allowed!
Required	No
Allow Zero Length	No
Indexed	No

If you look at the **Field Properties** in **Table Design View** you can use **Validation** to help. Validation makes sure that only data you want to be entered is allowed. Kate has made sure that the only entry allowed for the field 'County' is Fleetshire.

Microsoft Access

⚠ Only Fleetshire Allowed!

[OK] [Help]

If anything else is entered then the validation text appears on the screen in its own window.

This is a very simple example. You can write more complicated sentences. For example, if only Fleetshire, Stoneshire and Greenshire were acceptable, you could write: 'Fleetshire' or 'Stoneshire' or 'Greenshire'. You could then enter one of these three but no others would be allowed.

What other validation rules could be added for the other fields in the database?

Adding more fields

On occasions you may wish to add or take away fields in your tables. This may be because you no longer need a field because nobody ever fills it in or someone wants a new field to record some extra information.

A word of warning however, deleting fields also means that all the data in that field is deleted too. Adding a field may mean updating hundreds of records so that they are all the same.

It is therefore best that you think of all the fields you could possibly need and delete them if you do not use them. It is easier to delete than to add.

Inserting and deleting fields

Kate forgot to add the video name and the rental cost so she added these fields in. To do this she opened her table in **Design View** and used the mouse to click on one row where she wanted to have an extra field. It turned black.

Kate opened the **Edit** menu and selected **Insert row**. She now had a space where she could enter her new field name.

You can see that she has added the two extra fields to the database.

Table: Table1

Field Name	Data Type	Description
Name	Text	
Street	Text	
Town	Text	
County	Text	
Post Code	Text	
Video	Text	
Video In	Date/Time	
Video Out	Date/Time	
Cost	Currency	

Field Properties

Field Size	50
Format	
Input Mask	

Are there any more fields that you can think of that may need to be added?

On the next page you will look at ways of reorganising the data in the database so that it is more useful.

On the next page you will look at ways of reorganising the data in the database so that it is more useful.

WHAT YOU HAVE TO DO

1. **Complete the design of the table.**
2. **Use Input Masks where necessary.**
3. **Add or delete fields if you need to.**
4. **Add some validation rules.**

4. We ask the questions

On this page you will look at how you can question and sort out data in your database, so that it can be used productively.

Queries

Your database now contains a great deal of data. Even though it is reasonably well organised in a table format, it is still difficult to find information quickly. To help with this, **Access** has a useful tool – **Query**.

This tool enables you to make up new tables in any order you like and only look for certain items of data.

Query enables you to ask questions about your database. You could ask:

- How many people belong to the video club?
- Which videos have been rented out?
- Which videos are overdue?

Asking the right questions

James needs to know who has videos that are overdue and he creates a query that shows this information.

He used **F11** to bring up the **Access Navigator Window**, and clicked on **New**.

On the next window he did not use the Query Wizard but selected **New Query** instead.

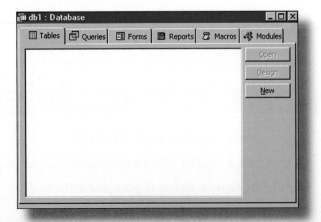

James now had to choose which table he wanted to ask questions about. This was easy as he only had one table – Video Shop Details.

He highlighted this using the mouse and clicked **OK**. Then he closed the **Add Table** window.

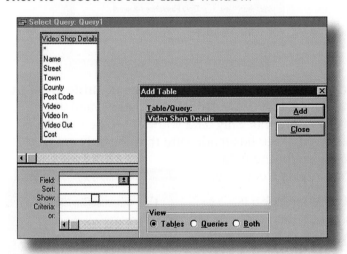

Construction work

James could now construct his query. He wanted to know who had not returned their rented videos. He needs a list of customers to whom he can write.

James created a new table of information that he wanted. First he double-clicked on the field names in the table to copy them to form a new table structure.

He used the pull-down menu to add the fields he wanted.

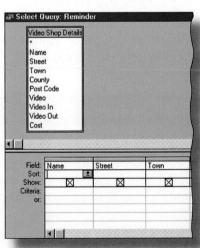

James then used **Criteria** to ensure that only the information he wanted was listed in his new table. The Criteria is simply what he wanted to look for. For example:

- in the **Name** he could type Smith – the query would list only people named Smith
- in the **Town** he could type Oldtown – the query would only find people who live in Oldtown.

James wanted to find overdue videos:

- Under **Video Out** he wrote in **<#13/12/99#** (today's date).

This tells the database only to look for entries where customers took out videos from 12/12/99 or before. This makes sure he does not list anyone who has recently rented out a video.

- Under **Video In** he typed **Is Null**.

This tells the database to look for entries where the **Video In** field is blank.

The query was complete.

James now used **View** and then **Datasheet** to see his new list.

When James was happy with his query, he closed the window.

He was asked if he wanted to save the changes that he had made, and he clicked **Yes**. He named his query in the **Save As** window and clicked **OK**.

James called his query **Reminder**. It is always a good idea to give Tables/Queries/Forms, names that say something about what they contain or do. As a database gets bigger you may have 10 tables and 20 queries – try guessing what query 18 does! 'Query 18' does not say anything about what it does. 'Reminder' as a name gives you a clue.

On the next page you will be using the reminder query to send out reminder letters to customers with overdue videos.

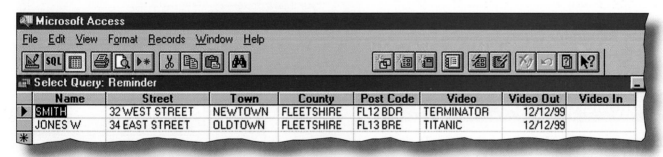

Name	Street	Town	County	Post Code	Video	Video Out	Video In
SMITH	32 WEST STREET	NEWTOWN	FLEETSHIRE	FL12 BDR	TERMINATOR	12/12/99	
JONES W	34 EAST STREET	OLDTOWN	FLEETSHIRE	FL13 BRE	TITANIC	12/12/99	

Finally, he clicked on **Sort** to put his table results in A to Z or Z to A order.

Show ■

When the cross in the square is shown then the field will be visible in the table. If you click on the cross then the field is not shown in your new table. Note that it is just hidden and not removed.

- Why do you think the **Is Null** is used? What would the query find if it were left blank?
- Can you think when you might not want to show certain fields on your new tables?

WHAT YOU HAVE TO DO

1. **Decide on a question to 'ask' your database.**
2. **Create a query to ask the question by using Criteria.**
3. **Create some other queries that will be useful for the video shop.**

5. Mail Merge

On this page you will see how you can use Mail Merge to save time and effort in writing to many people about the same topic. You will need to use a word processing package for this.

Using your completed database

You have constructed a database. Next you need to use the database together with **word processing** software to create a **Mail Merge**.

Using Mail Merge

A **Mail Merge** allows you to take the information in your database and produce reminders for videos that are overdue. The software will automatically make the links between the database and the word processing software.

Zoë is using the **Reminder Query** to send a letter to all customers that have overdue videos.

Using Mail Merge Helper in Word

Zoë opened Microsoft **Word**. She went to **Tools** and clicked on **Mail Merge**.

Mail Merge Helper appeared. This showed the three steps required to complete a Mail Merge.

Zoë clicked on **Create** and then **Form Letters**.

On the next window displayed she picked **New** followed by **Main Document**.

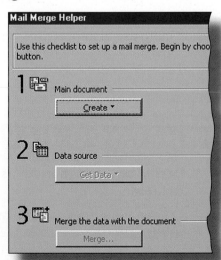

Get your data

Zoë was now ready to find the data that would make up her letters.

She clicked on **Get Data** and then **Open Data Source**.

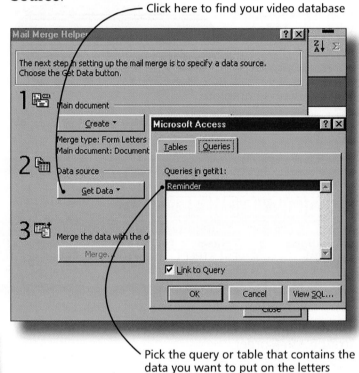

Click here to find your video database

Pick the query or table that contains the data you want to put on the letters

Zoë needed to find the video database. She selected your database file. Zoë has selected **Reminder** from the Queries table.

Word told her that it could not find any merge fields and asked if she wanted to edit the main document now. She clicked on **Yes**.

Insert Merge Fields

Zoë inserted the merge fields where she wanted them to appear on her document.

She placed the flashing cursor where she wanted her merge field to appear.

On the **Mail Merge** tool bar she picked **Insert Merge Field** and picked the field she wanted to put on her letter.

The merge fields appeared like this **<<Name>>**.

Zoë made sure she left spaces between the merge fields and the normal text.

Finally, Zoë checked the way that the letter was set out and how the merge fields were used.

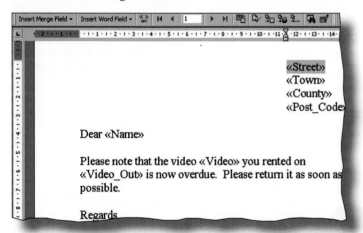

It is possible to insert the merge fields more than once if you need to.

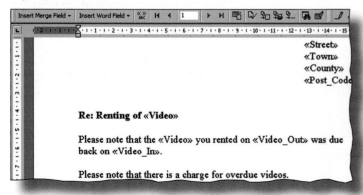

You can see that in this example the merge field **<<Video>>** has been used twice.

Merge your document

On the tool bar there are two merge buttons. One sends the merge documents straight to the printer, the other to a file so that you can see what you have created. It is best to merge to another file just to check what it looks like before you print.

Zoë clicked on the **Merge to New Document** button. This created a new **Word** File with the merged data.

Look at the three letters Zoë has merged from her database. Can you spot the merged fields?

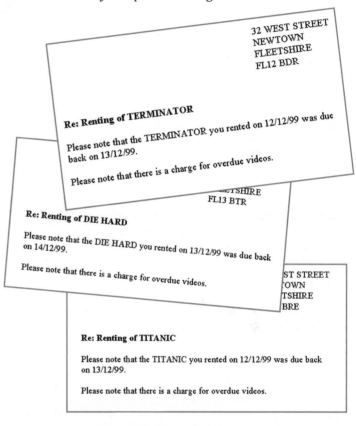

On the next page you will look at ways of using the data in your database together with spreadsheets to provide more useful information for the video shop.

WHAT YOU HAVE TO DO

1. **Open a word processing package and use the Mail Merge facility to open a database file.**
2. **Create a Mail Merge document using Merge Fields.**
3. **Merge the document with the data in your database to create a Mail Merge.**

6. Accounting for the future

In the next part of this unit you will be looking at how spreadsheets can help make sure the video shop can make a profit.

Accounts

The owners of the video shop are not making enough money and they are worried that they may have to close the shop down. Now Zoë and her friends are going to use spreadsheets to see why it is not making any money.

What's happening?

Zoë, James and Kate have input all the financial data into a spreadsheet so that they can see what is happening.

- What do you think is happening?
- What do you think of the layout of the spreadsheet?
- List some things you like about the spreadsheet.

Clear as a bell

Zoë decided to use some formatting features to make sure that the data was easy to read.

First she wanted to make the title large and clear. To do this she clicked on the cell **A1** (where the title was), and increased the size of the typeface.

To apply some shading Zoë highlighted the block of cells A4 to A6. On the formatting tool bar she clicked on **Fill color**. There were lots of colours to choose from.

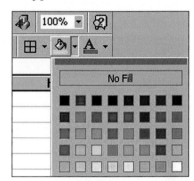

Zoë needed to experiment first – not all of the colours went well with each other. For example, she tried using really dark colours with black text.

She clicked on the **Font color** which is next to Fill color, to choose the colour of the text.

Leaving the cells highlighted she used the **Borders** button to insert a grid around her figures.

Finally, Zoë picked light green and grey to make the spreadsheet stand out. The negative numbers appeared in red, which made them easy to spot – red means danger!

	A	B	C	D	E	F	G
1	**The Video Shop**						
2							
3		APR	MAY	JUN	JUL	AUG	SEP
4	Rent	£250.00	£250.00	£250.00	£250.00	£250.00	£250.00
5	Wages	£400.00	£450.00	£400.00	£425.00	£400.00	£475.00
6	Purchases	£1,000.00	£1,200.00	£1,300.00	£1,250.00	£1,100.00	£1,200.00
7	Costs	£1,650.00	£1,900.00	£1,950.00	£1,925.00	£1,750.00	£1,925.00
8							
9	Sales	£1,701.00	£1,862.00	£1,841.00	£1,818.00	£1,841.00	£1,940.00
10							
11	Profit	£51.00	-£38.00	-£109.00	-£107.00	£91.00	£15.00

Microsoft Excel - Video shop 1
File Edit View Insert Format Tools Data Window Help

Format Cells

The rent, wages and videos bought to rent out (i.e. the Purchases) need to be displayed in a currency format with a pound sign.

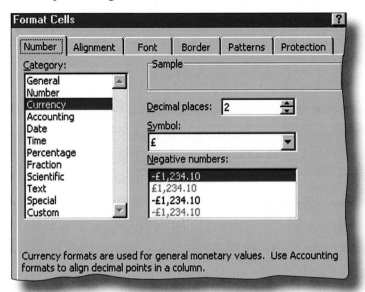

To set this up Kate highlighted the block of cells B4 to G6. She opened the **Format** menu and clicked on **Cells**. Then she clicked on **Number** on the file cards and on **Currency** from the category list. Finally, she clicked on the **Negative number** format that she wanted displayed, and then on **OK**.

Working it out

Zoë then added up the running costs of the business.

● Can you think where **formulas** have been used to calculate the costs?

Look at the formulas used.

3		APR		MAY
4	Rent	250		250
5	Wages	400		450
6	Purchases	1000		1200
7	Costs	=SUM(B4:B6)		=SUM(C4:C6)

Remember that you can copy cells with formulas in them. They will automatically adjust to ensure that calculations made in the columns and rows are correct.

● What has changed in the formulas for the costs in April and May?

Turning the page

Microsoft **Excel** allows you to have more than one page to your spreadsheet. Think of it like this book, divided into chapters to make it easier to read. The pages can be seen at the bottom of the screen.

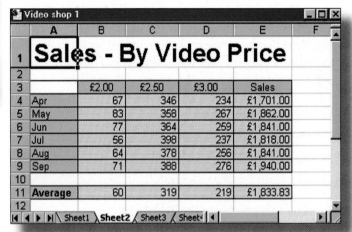

Click on Sheet 2 and a new page appears.

There can be as many as 255 sheets in one **Excel** file so there is a great deal of space to work with!

Zoë, Kate and James calculated the total of video rental money collected each month using **Sheet 2**.

Kate copied the rental collected figures into Sheet 2. She used the same formatting styles and colours that Zoë used for Sheet 1 to enter the **Sales** figures.

● Why do you think that this is important? Does it matter what colours or font sizes you use?

On the next page you will see how Zoë and James calculated the rentals collected.

WHAT YOU HAVE TO DO

1. **Copy the spreadsheet figures of the video shop.**

2. **Format the cells using the buttons on the formatting tool bar.**

3. **Enter the calculated values for the Costs and the Profit.**

4. **Open Sheet 2 and copy the number of video rentals made over the six month period.**

7. Sale now on

Next you will build up our spreadsheet to show the details of where the money for the video shop is coming from.

Calculating sales

Zoë and her friends used the different **Sheets** available to build up a model to show what happens when different videos are rented. If they can find out how many videos need to be rented to make a profit then the video shop owners can use this information. Here you will see how they have used **Absolute Cell Referencing** and **averages** to help them.

Absolute Cell Referencing

Zoë needed to calculate the **Rentals** in the spreadsheet. What formula would she use? She calculated the rentals figures using **Absolute Cell Referencing**. This isn't as complicated as it sounds.

When you copy formulas, the row and columns adjust automatically to give the correct results. Sometimes you may not want this to happen because the wrong results will be calculated. The way to stop this from happening is to use Absolute Cell Referencing.

Zoë needed to multiply the cost in row 3 by the number of videos in rows 4 to 9. To save time she copied the formula:
=(B3*B4)+(C3*C4)+(D3*D4)

to the next row down and got
=(B4*B5)+(C4*C5)+(D4*D5).

● Try this out – you will get some strange results!

What Zoë needed to do was to **lock** the cells in row 3 so that they did not change when she copied down the formula. She locked the formula by typing in two $ symbols:
=B3

Zoë did the same with the other two parts of the formula, and copied the formula down using the mouse.

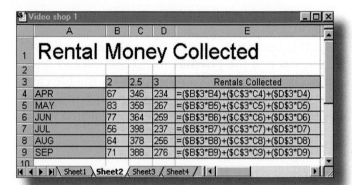

Average

You are used to seeing totals at the bottom of tables of figures. In the table below there is something different. The **average** number of videos and the average rentals over the last 6 months have been calculated.

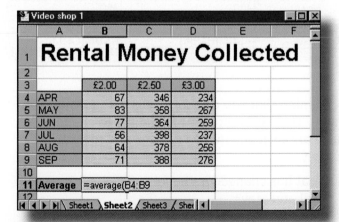

To do this Zoë clicked on a cell where she wanted the answer to her calculation to appear. She typed

=AVERAGE(

and dragged the mouse over the cells B4 to B9 that she wished to average. The cells were automatically entered into the equation for her.

Finally, she entered this formula into the other cells. She did this quickly and easily using just the mouse.

Viewing cells in different worksheets ■

Zoë thought it would be useful to see the rentals collected on Sheet 1 so that she could subtract them from the costs and find out if the shop would make a profit.

Zoë was able to display the rentals collected figures in Sheet 2 on Sheet 1. Here is how she did it.

She added a new row labelled 'Rentals Collected' , using the same formats. Then she went to Sheet 1 clicked on cell B9, and typed =. Finally she clicked on Sheet 2 and went to cell E4, and then pressed **Enter**.

The rentals collected figure was now displayed in Sheet 1. She then did the same for the rentals collected figures for the other 5 months.

By adding a row for the profits and using the formulas shown Zoë was able to calculate how much money the video shop would make each month.

Making financial models ■

Note that Zoë had not copied the rentals figure from Sheet 2 to Sheet 1. She was just **viewing** the rentals figures in Sheet 2 on Sheet 1.

● Click on Sheet 2
● Change some of the video rentals numbers in rows 4 to 9

What happens to the rentals figures on Sheet 2?

● Click on Sheet 1

What has happened to the rentals figures on Sheet 1?

What has happened to the profits on Sheet 1?

Zoë had now created a way of being able to see what happens when the amounts of differing video rentals are changed. The term for creating these *What if...?* experiments is called **modelling**.

Financial models are useful for making quick and easy projections to the overall effects on final profits and losses when individual figures are changed. They save a great deal of re-calculation!

On the next page you will see how Zoë went on to use Sheets 3 and Sheet 4 to set up a model using the spreadsheets already created in her attempt to help the video shop owners try and find a solution to their troubles.

	A	B	C	D	E	F	G
1	The Video Shop						
2							
3		APR	MAY	JUN	JUL	AUG	SEP
4	Rent	£250.00	£250.00	£250.00	£250.00	£250.00	£250.00
5	Wages	£400.00	£450.00	£400.00	£425.00	£400.00	£475.00
6	Purchases	£1,000.00	£1,200.00	£1,300.00	£1,250.00	£1,100.00	£1,200.00
7	Costs	£1,650.00	£1,900.00	£1,950.00	£1,925.00	£1,750.00	£1,925.00
8							
9	Rentals Collected	£1,701.00					
10							
11	Profit	=B9-B7					
12							
13							

Sheet1 / Sheet2 / Sheet3 / Sheet4

WHAT YOU HAVE TO DO

1. Copy Sheet 2 (the Rentals Collected information), using the same format as Sheet 1.

2. Enter Absolute Cell References in formulas to calculate rentals collected totals.

3. Enter Cell references from Sheet 2 to view rental collections in Sheet 1.

4. Enter a profit row and formula to calculate how much money the video shop is making.

5. Try out your spreadsheet to see if the values change.

8. A new model

On this page James is looking at using a spreadsheet model to tell the video shop owners what they need to rent out to make the most amount of money.

What if...?

Zoë and James used Sheets 1 and 2 to show what was happening in the business and how much profit it was making. They now want to investigate what they need to rent out to make the most profit. They will need to undertake some spreadsheet modelling. This means that they will predict how much profit they can make by constructing 'What if...?' questions using the spreadsheet.

Sheets 3 and 4

Zoë and James wanted to use Sheets 3 and 4 to predict future profits. To do this they first needed to get copies of Sheets 1 and 2 and put them in Sheets 3 and 4.

James clicked on Sheet 1 and highlighted the cell block A1 to G11. Then he used the **Copy** function to copy the cells. He clicked on Sheet 3 and pasted them into cell A.

He switched to Sheet 3, went to A1 and added the word **Forecasting** so he did not get Sheet 1 and Sheet 3 muddled up.

A	B	C	D	E
The Video Shop - Forecasting				

Then James clicked on Sheet 2 and highlighted the cell block A1 to E11. He used the **Copy** function to copy the cells. Then he clicked on Sheet 4 and pasted into cell A1.

Finally, on Sheet 4 he went to cell A1 and added the word **Forecasting** so he did not get Sheet 2 and Sheet 4 muddled up.

Setting up the model

James had to change the cell references that refer to Sheet 2 on Sheet 3. The Rentals Collected displayed in cell B9 were still those from Sheet 2.

		APR
Rent	250	
Wages	400	
Purchases	1000	
Costs	=SUM(B4:B6)	
Rentals Collected	=Sheet2!E4	
Profit	=B9-B7	

Sheet1 / Sheet2 \ **Sheet3**

James clicked on Cell B9 and typed **=**. Then he went to Sheet 4 and clicked on cell E4, and pressed **Enter**. He repeated this for cells E5 to E9.

James then cleared the numbers showing how many videos were rented out on Sheet 4. To do this he clicked on Sheet 4, highlighted the block of cells B4 to D9 and used **Clear Contents** from the **Edit** menu.

● What has happened to the totals in the Rentals Collected column?

● What has happened to the Average row?

Video shop 1

	A	B	C	D	E	F	G
1	**Rentals Collected - Forecast**						
2							
3		£2.00	£2.50	£3.00	Sales		
4	Apr				£0.00		
5	May				£0.00		
6	Jun				£0.00		
7	Jul				£0.00		
8	Aug				£0.00		
9	Sep				£0.00		
10							
11	Average	#DIV/0!	#DIV/0!	#DIV/0!	£0.00		
12							

Sheet1 / Sheet2 / Sheet3 \ **Sheet4**

 Absolute Cell Referencing *p123* Making financial models *p123*

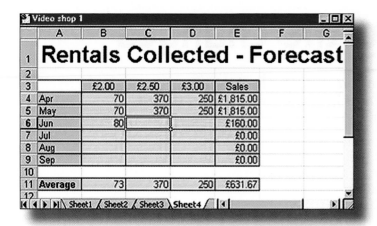

James entered the video rental numbers that he thought should be possible. James then looked on Sheet 3 to see if his predictions were acceptable. He compared the profits on Sheet 1 with the predicted profits on Sheet 3.

7	Costs	£1,650.00	£1,900.00	£1,950.00	£1,925.00	£1,750.00	£1,925.00
8							
9	Rentals Collected	£1,900.00	£1,950.00	£1,970.00	£1,970.00	£1,950.00	£1,950.00
10							
11	Profit		£250.00	£50.00	£20.00	£45.00	£200.00	£25.00

Sheet1 / Sheet2 \ Sheet3 / Sheet4 /

7	Costs	£1,650.00	£1,900.00	£1,950.00	£1,925.00	£1,750.00	£1,925.00
8							
9	Rentals Collected	£1,701.00	£1,862.00	£1,841.00	£1,818.00	£1,841.00	£1,940.00
10							
11	Profit	£51.00	-£38.00	-£109.00	-£107.00	£91.00	£15.00

Sheet1 / Sheet2 / Sheet3 / Sheet4 /

You can do some more modelling by changing other figures on Sheet 3.

- The wages are based upon two people working in the store – What would happen if there was only one person? (Hint – halve the wages.)

- The video store buys its videos from Videos Direct. Wholesale Videos are 10% cheaper. Use the spreadsheet to recalculate the purchases.

In answering these questions you can see that the spreadsheet is a powerful tool when used to predict future ideas. Remember this is known as **modelling**.

Protection

Sheet 1 contains all the data that needed to be viewed to make decisions about what to rent. The majority of this data had been collected from Sheets 2, 3 and 4.

James did not need to make changes to Sheet 1 to alter the data shown. To stop anyone from changing Sheet 1 by mistake he decided to **protect** Sheet 1.

James used the **Tools** menu and clicked on **Protection**.

In the dialogue box that appeared he clicked on **Protect Sheet**.

You can add a password if you want – this can be dangerous since you may forget it and there is no way around it if you do!

On the next page you will look at using **Reports** to display information so that it can be even more easily understood.

WHAT YOU HAVE TO DO

1. **Copy Sheet 1 to Sheet 3.**

2. **Copy Sheet 2 to Sheet 4.**

3. **Clear the rentals collected figures from Sheet 3 and replace them with relative cell references from Sheet 2.**

4. **Clear the video rental details from Sheet 4.**

5. **Experiment with altering the values in Sheet 4 to see the changes in Sheet 3.**

9. Charting the changes

On the last page of this unit you will be looking at different ways to change and present your data so that it is easier to see what is going on.

Making changes

There are two ways in which you can enhance your work:

- **Graphs**
- **Reports.**

Report Wizards were covered in Skills Book 2. Look these up again to refresh your memory.

Zoë has been looking at changing the standard format of the reports. Let's look at how she changed the design.

Change a report

The reminder query form shown on page 117 was used to construct a report. It now needs to be changed since the address is no longer required on the report. This is because it is kept in the shop and not sent to anyone.

Zoë could change the report by either moving or deleting fields to achieve the desired result. She clicked on the report she wanted to change in the main Database Window. Then she clicked on **Design**. She could only make changes to her report when she was in this view.

To delete or move fields she first selected them by putting the mouse pointer over the field and clicking with the mouse button.

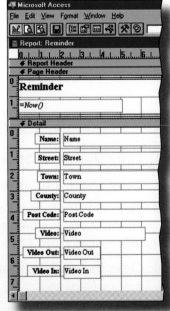

Zoë needed to remove the Street, Town, County, and Post Code fields as they were not required. She used the Delete key to remove the fields that had been selected. By holding down the Shift key she could select as many items as she wanted.

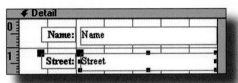

Removing the fields has left an unwanted gap. Zoë used the mouse to drag the **Video In** and **Video out** fields up. Then she used the pointer to select the Video Out and Video In fields. As she moved the pointer over the items she had selected a black hand appeared instead of the pointer. She clicked and dragged the items up to close up the gap.

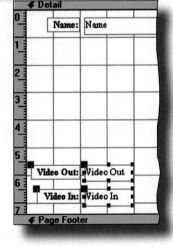

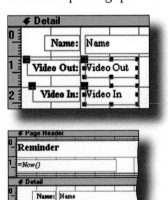

Zoë clicked on the **Page Footer** and moved the pointer until it changed to a double-headed arrow. Then she dragged the page footer up to remove the space left by deleting the unwanted items.

Finally, she clicked on **Print Preview** on the tool bar to view the new report.

You can change other things on your report in design view.

Add a company logo or chart ∎

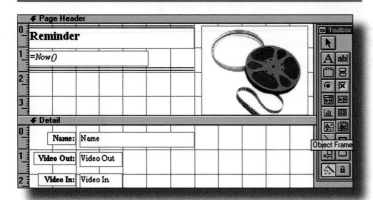

To make their work look more professional, Zoë decided she would add a graphic image. To do this she opened the report in **Design View** and clicked on **Toolbox** on the main tool bar. She clicked on **Object Frame** and clicked and dragged the pointer to where she wanted the image to appear.

She selected a software package from the list displayed and found the image file she wanted to insert.

Amend a report title ∎

Not all of the objects are fields, some are **Labels**.

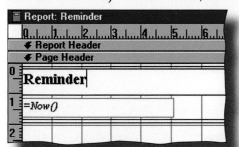

Because Zoë has changed the report it is no longer a reminder sent out to people but a reference for staff in the shop. She decided to change *Reminder* to *Video Rental*.

First she opened the report in **Design View** and used the pointer to select the Reminder label. Then she clicked on the label again. She was then able to edit the text in much the same way as she would when using a basic word processing package. She deleted *Reminder* and typed in *Video Rental*.

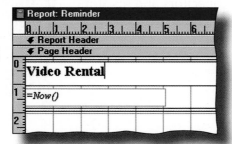

Zoë was pleased with her efforts in changing the reports. However, she did notice that when she changed the size of the 'Video' field half of the information was missing.

On the report in the **Design View** it looked OK – Video fitted in nicely.

However, on the preview the field should have said 'Terminator' but all that came out was Termina.

Make sure that you check your report thoroughly for any errors before you print it out.

On Target

You should now know how to use databases, spreadsheets and word processing to:

- edit and change **Database Form** layouts
- use **Queries** to interrogate your database
- use **Mail Merge** in word processing
- use multiple sheets and **Absolute Cell Referencing** in spreadsheets.

WHAT YOU HAVE TO DO

1. **Create graphs and reports from the database and spreadsheets.**
2. **Change the details on the reports in Design View.**
3. **Put command buttons on your spreadsheets.**
4. **Read the IT at work case study on the next page.**

IT at work

Kingshill Electronic Products is an electronics and electro-mechanical engineering company which designs and makes electrical power supplies. Here we see how they use a database and other ICT applications.

What is a transformer?

Electrical equipment runs on different voltages. For example, a Game Boy operates on 3V. The black box that is plugged into the mains is a **power supply**. It converts 240V to just 3V.

Kingshill design and build standard and special power supplies. This means that the customer tells them:

- where the power supply will be installed
- how much voltage and current is needed going in
- how much voltage and current is needed coming out.

Kingshill take all these factors into consideration and decide if it is possible to build the power supply that the customer wants. Then they design, construct and assemble it.

KINGSHILL

Design and build

Design

When Kingshill have agreed to build the power supply they set about designing it. They use a computer and special software to design the circuit boards for the power supply.

Construct

The circuit board is a special fibreglass board that electrical components such as capacitors and resistors can be soldered onto.

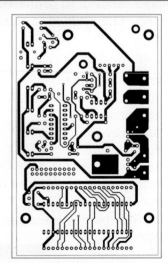

Some of the power supplies deal with dangerously high voltages and are required to have protective metal cases that the circuit boards can be put in. Kingshill design and make these boxes too.

Large computer-controlled cutting and stamping machines are used to make the cases from sheet steel.

Assembly

Kingshill have teams of people who are responsible for the construction of the power supplies. They follow the design drawings created by the design teams.

Test

Every power supply is tested to make sure that:

- it does what the customer wants it to do
- it is safe to use
- there are no assembly faults.

Kingshill have invested in IT to help them keep one step ahead of their competitors.

- Design work takes place on a computer.
- Assembly drawings are made on a computer.
- Information and ordering is completed using computers.
- Manufacturing and testing is completed using computers.

They use a large database to help them keep track of all the components that they need for each job.

Each job has a 'Kit' list, that the design team creates. This details:

- every component required to build the power supply
- the cost of each component
- the overall cost.

The people who order the components can also view this database, and place the necessary orders when the construction teams need to assemble the power supplies. This means that components are ordered only when they are needed and Kingshill do not have to keep large quantities of electrical components sitting on their shelves.

All the costings are put into a spreadsheet for the Finance Director. He can then monitor expenditure in the company.

P Series Product Costings

Product No.	P300	P400	P500	P600
Labour cost	£25.50	£30.25	£34.08	£37.66
Material cost	£122.34	£161.23	£191.79	£220.55
Total production cost	**£147.84**	**£191.48**	**£225.87**	**£258.21**
Variable costs				
Electricity	£1.10	£1.25	£1.30	£1.40
Gas	£0.30	£0.35	£0.43	£0.45
Water	£0.20	£0.21	£0.24	£0.24
Transport	£0.12	£0.12	£0.12	£0.12
Other	£1.25	£1.28	£1.30	£1.32
Total variable costs	£2.97	£3.21	£3.39	£3.53
Contribution to fixed costs				
Salaries	£15.03	£15.16	£15.23	£15.50
Pensions	£1.50	£1.51	£1.52	£1.55
Rent	£20.87	£21.66	£22.03	£22.03
Rates	£5.54	£5.54	£5.54	£5.54
Insc.	£3.10	£3.10	£3.10	£3.10
Company car	£12.22	£12.22	£12.22	£12.22
petrol/oil	£6.08	£6.08	£6.08	£6.08
Other	£25.82	£25.82	£25.82	£25.82
Total fixed costs	£90.16	£91.09	£91.54	£91.84
Total all costs	**£240.97**	**£285.78**	**£320.80**	**£353.58**
Selling price	**£387.00**	**£442.00**	**£490.00**	**£572.00**
Estimated net profit per unit	**£146.03**	**£156.22**	**£169.20**	**£218.42**
Profit as % of selling price	37.7%	35.3%	34.5%	38.2%

Page 1

7 Bringing IT Together

By now you should have a good grasp of a wide range of computer software packages. Can you apply what you know to solve some problems using ICT?

On Target

In this final unit you will be asked to use ICT to solve a problem. You will need to use more than one application in this work.

This page will guide you through the sort of things you will need to do. Pages 132–135 take you through a specific example, showing how a group of pupils worked together to create a web site.

Finally, pages 136–143 will guide you through a number of possible projects you could try. Your teacher may tell you which one to do, or maybe give you a choice.

What's the problem?

Before you start work, make sure you understand exactly what the problem is you have been asked to solve. Do you know:

● who the problem affects?
● where the problem is?
● what ICT equipment is available?
● what software and hardware you are likely to need?
● how you will present your ideas and solution?

You may have clear answers to some or all of these questions, but the chances are you will need to find out some more information.

Investigation

Where might you go to find the information you need? You might find it useful to look at and evaluate a similar existing solution. This might involve:

● visiting the school and/or local library
● searching CD-ROMs and the Internet
● talking to an existing user
● visiting the location.

First thoughts

As you start to think of some possible ways to solve the problem, start to make notes, sketches, draw systems diagrams, etc. on paper rather than at the computer. Ask lots of questions:

● Who...?   ● When...?
● How much...?   ● How many...?
● How often...?   ● Where...?
● What if...?   ● Why...?

Planning

Again, planning should be done on paper, rather than on screen.

- What do you need to do first? What can't be done until something else has been?
- Are all the resources readily available, or will anything have to be specially obtained?
- When can you test ideas out?
- How much time have you got?
- If you are working in a team, who is doing what and when?

Working at the computer

Here's where you need to use your computer skills to their full effect. You may need to learn some new tricks too! Ask if the manuals are available for the programs you will be using, or use the **Help** button.

Transferring data between software packages can cause problems. It may be that the work you do will need to be opened on another computer. Always check this out in good time. What works on one computer may not work in the same way on another.

Evaluation

Remember to keep checking and evaluating your work as it progresses, as well as when it's finally complete. For example:

- When you have reached a particular stage, run the program and check to see that it all works as intended.
- Discuss your program with a friend to see if they can follow how to use it.
- Compare different possible solutions, and decide which is the best approach.
- Ask someone who will use the system to try it out, maybe with particular reference to a part of it you are not sure about.

Final presentation

- Who is the audience for the presentation?
- Where will it be and when?
- What illustrations should the report include?
- What are the key points that need to be communicated?
- How are any 'further developments' going to be explained?

WHAT YOU HAVE TO DO

Read this page, and the case study on the next two pages. As you work through your own project refer back to this material and try to apply it yourself.

Movie magic (I)

A group of pupils used the Internet to invite answers to their survey to discover what people's favourite films were.

On-line survey

As an end of term project a class was asked to carry out a survey. The class was divided into groups, and each group was given this briefing:

> 'The people who run an art centre have decided to have a film season. They have asked you to find out which films are most popular.'

One group decided to use their school web site to run the survey. They asked their teacher if that was OK, and he agreed.

In this section you will look at the work they did.

What's the big idea?

Lisa, Jake, Susie, Nathan, Asha and Duane sat round and discussed the project. First they thought about whether they would need any more information about what was required. They decided the brief was clear, and they could make a start immediately.

They thought it would be a good idea to write down a clear statement of what they were going to do.

The question they decided to ask was:

> **What is the best film you have ever seen?**

> **What we are going to do**
>
> We have decided to put our survey question on a web page. We will design a page that has one question on it.
>
> We will include an e-mail link. Everyone who sees the page can easily send us an e-mail answer to the question. We will collect all the e-mail answers that we receive.
>
> Finally we will work out the number of people who gave each answer and make a report with graphs in it to show the results of our survey.

Planning

Next, the group sat down and thought of all the tasks they would have to complete, and what software packages would help them.

> **Tasks**
> Collect images
> Enter text
> Format layout and appearance
> Create graphs
> Write reports
> Enter links
> Receive e-mail
> Present results
> Collect answers
> Create web page
> Work out results

Here is the list of tasks they drew up. After that, they chose the software packages they would use for each task.

> **Packages**
> FrontPage Editor
> Web browser
> E-mail package
> Spreadsheet
> Word processor

In all, they had to use five different software packages to complete the project.

Although they decided to work together, they all agreed to take on a particular responsibility for a different job.

> **Responsibilities**
> Lisa - Find the illustrations
> Jake and Susie - Develop the web site.
> Nathan - Collect the survey replies
> Asha - Put the replies into a spreadsheet
> Duane - write the final report for the Arts Centre

Find illustrations

Lisa had the job of finding illustrations for the web site.

- She searched the Internet using a search engine.
- She looked on CD-ROMs.

Here are some of the things she had to keep in mind while she searched:

- The illustrations had to be about films.
- The illustration couldn't be about any particular film (because that might bias the survey results).
- She had to be careful about copyright.
- The illustrations should be interesting and attractive.

She found several pictures and showed them to the rest of the group. They picked their favourites.

The teacher used **FrontPage Editor** to import the chosen graphics files to the school Internet server.

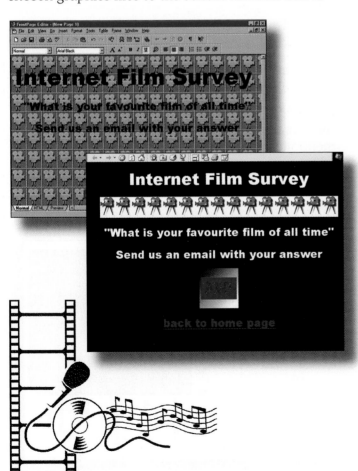

Create the web site

Jake and Susie had the job of using **FrontPage Editor** to make the web site structure and enter the text and illustrations.

- They had to type in the page title, question and instructions.
- They had to create a page layout.
- They had to pick colours and fonts.
- They had to include the illustrations, either as graphics or as background.

On the top left is their first attempt at the web page design.

The whole group looked at this design and shared their ideas. Here was what they said.

- It is eye-catching.
- It does make you think about 'films'.
- It is too cluttered.
- It is hard to read.
- People might not be able to understand it.

They decided to try a different design instead. On the bottom left is the second design they made.

Movie Magic (2)

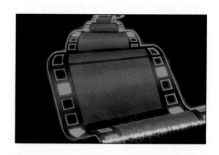

Going live

The teacher posted the survey page to the school web server. He also created a link from the school home page to the survey page.

To make sure that they received lots of replies to their survey the pupils did the following:

● They told their family and friends about it and asked them to reply to the survey.

● They put a poster up in the school corridor.

● They wrote to a local radio station to tell people about the survey.

Replies

It was Nathan's job to collect the survey replies. He created a link on the web page, with his school e-mail address.

Send us an email with y...

click here to reply

As the results came in he saved and printed out all the e-mails. He passed the results on to Asha, whose job was to work out results.

Potential problem

It is important to think of what might go wrong with your project, and how to solve any problems. For example, Nathan complained that reading all the e-mails was a big job. He thought he wouldn't have time to do it all. To solve this problem the other people in the group agreed that they would all help him.

Working out problems and making sure that nobody feels unhappy about the way the project is developing is an important part of the task.

Results and report

It was Asha's job to collect the results in a spreadsheet. She:

● entered the names of the most popular films into the spreadsheet and the number of people who mentioned each film

● worked out the percentage of people mentioning each film and turned them into graphs

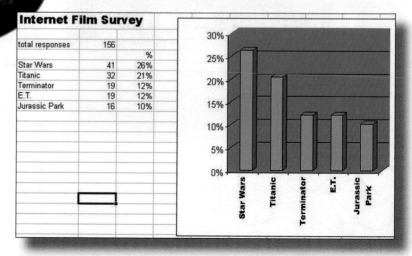

Internet Film Survey

total responses	156	
		%
Star Wars	41	26%
Titanic	32	21%
Terminator	19	12%
E.T.	19	12%
Jurassic Park	16	10%

Writing the report

Duane had the job of writing the report. First he thought about the **purpose** of the report and who the **audience** would be. He read the results, and then wrote about them in his own words. He used a word processor to enter the text. He added the graphs as illustrations to the report.

The report was then ready for the Arts Centre.

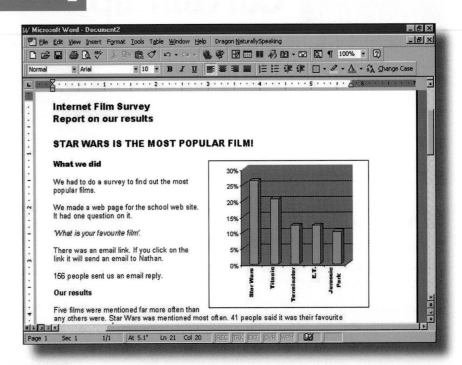

More ideas

The web survey was so successful that the group decided to do some follow-up work for their next ICT project. Here are the further tasks they did:

- Wrote an article about the web survey for the school magazine.
- Took the survey web page off the school web site, because they didn't want to receive any more answers to their survey. In its place they created a new web page, showing the results of the survey.
- Sent an e-mail to everyone who had joined in the survey. In the e-mail they thanked them for taking part, and told them the URL of the site where the survey results appeared.

Even if you don't have time to do follow-up work, it is a good idea to write down your ideas about other work that you could do if you had time. This is part of your evaluation.

Curtain up

It's nearly time for the school play. You might be surprised at the part ICT could take!

The prologue

Your school is about to stage a performance of The Mikado. How could ICT be used to help? For example, it could help in:

- producing a range of graphic items, such as posters, leaflets and programme notes
- creating a series of web pages for cast members, and to promote the event on the school web site
- designing the set and costumes
- controlling a series of special effects
- organising ticket sales.

You need to present your proposals to the drama department for their consideration.

If you prefer, you can choose another play to do the design for.

Planning

If you are working on your own or with a partner you will need to choose which of the following tasks and applications you are going to do. If you are part of a group, divide the tasks up between you.

- To create graphic items, you will mainly need to use **Draw** or **Paint** programs, **DTP** or a **word processor**. Can they be printed out and copied in colour?
- To produce web pages to go on your school's Intranet you will need to use a web editor or a graphics/DTP package that has the facility to convert pages to html.
- To design the set and/or costumes you will need access to some **3D CAD** packages. Have you enough experience at using these?
- To set off special effects on stage you will need a control system package.
- To develop a system for booking tickets you will need a database and spreadsheet package.

Investigation

You will need to get hold of a copy of the play being performed. Make sure you have a basic idea of:

- the plot
- who the main characters are
- where and when the play is set.

Depending on which tasks you are doing you may need to find out more about the period the play is set in. Look in the library and use the Internet to discover the sorts of colours, patterns, textures and images that might be appropriate. Print these images out to use as a reference.

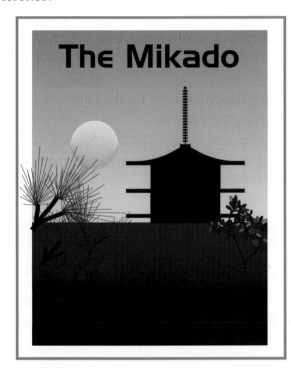

First thoughts

Here are just a few questions to get you going. You should be able to think of many more.

- Who would use the systems you create?
- When would they be needed by?
- How many copies of the poster and programme would be needed?
- How often will the play be performed?
- Where will tickets be sold from?

Working at the computer

Developing graphics

If you are using a graphics program to design a poster, you will need to think about the following:

- What font and size will the name of the play be created in?
- What other information will need to be included on the poster?
- What images could be used to attract people's attention? Will they be clip art, photographs or specially drawn?
- What other graphic devices, e.g. lines, colours, patterns, shapes could be used?
- What size will it be printed? Which printer will be used?

Evaluation

You will probably come up with a number of variations for the poster – maybe different colour schemes, layouts, images, typefaces, etc.

Print some of these out and show them to people. Ask them some key questions:

- Can they read the title of the play?
- Does it give them an idea of the time and place the play is set in, and what sort of play it is? (e.g. mystery, comedy, tragedy, musical.)
- Does it encourage them to attend?
- Can they tell when it's due to be performed?

Sports day

How well run is your school's sports day?

Could it be improved with a greater use of ICT?

The problem

Make a series of proposals to use ICT to improve your school's sports day.

International athletics meetings like the Olympic Games use a wide range of ICT applications to do things like:

- provide highly sophisticated timing systems to measure and record the athletes' performances
- keep the audience informed of current events, scores, timings, etc
- organise the programme of events across a range of locations and days
- provide ticket booking services
- produce graphic materials to promote the events.

Investigation

You will need to talk to whoever is responsible for organising your school's sports day. Find out how the following are done, and the extent to which ICT is used:

- Planning the programme for the day.
- Advertising the event.
- Recording performances as they happen.
- Keeping a record of performances on the day, and previous records.

First thoughts

You will need to decide what you are going to try and achieve. At this stage you should be aiming to produce some things to show whoever organises the sports day how ICT might be used. Following are some possibilities:

Before the event

To make sure that the event is well attended it needs to be advertised. Posters can be designed using a graphics package.

Sketch out ideas first and get other people's opinions about which design is best. Try to balance visual impact with the essential information the poster should convey.

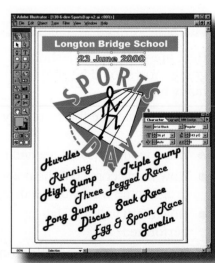

What's on the programme?

A printed programme of the events could be made using either a word processing or DTP package.

The front cover would need a visual impact celebrating sporting achievement within the school. Inside it would need to be set out like a table, showing a list of all the events with the time, place and other details.

The common format for this would be A5-sized pages printed side by side on an A4 sheet, and photocopied or printed on both sides. Most DTP packages will be able to create a template for this format.

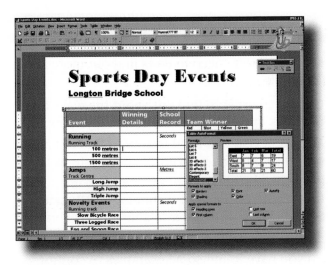

On the day

A portable computer could be used to enter the sports day results as they happen. A spreadsheet package would be ideally suited for this job. It should have the list of events already entered and columns headed 'First', 'Second', 'Third' set out in order to enter the names, teams and times. These could be pasted in from the package used to create the printed programme.

Not only would this be an easy way to record the results, but if the school has competing teams, the spreadsheet could be used to calculate the points awarded and the overall winners.

Instant recall

A digital camera could be used to capture pictures of the main events. The pictures taken on the day can be loaded into a computer and then pasted into a web page using an HTML editor. A database package could be used to store the names and winning performances so that they can be easily looked up in the future.

Congratulations!

Finally, the school may want to celebrate the achievement of the successful athletes with winners' certificates.

These can be made using a graphics or DTP package. Ask your teacher if your school has any special paper for printing certificates. Special pre-printed packs can look a lot more professional.

You will then need to work out how to print them with the winners' names and event details.

Working at the computer ▪

When you've decided which ICT programs you are going to use you will need to check that the necessary hardware and software will be available when you need it, both before, during and after sports day. If you are planning to exchange data between packages or machines, try the process out in advance to make sure it works without problems.

Presentation ▪

Remember, your aim is to convince the organiser of sports day that your ideas should be used. Plan how you will present your work as clearly as possible.

- What are the benefits?
- What are the costs?
- What problems might there be?

Spring time

Can you advise a water-bottling company how to improve their quality control systems?

Bottling out

A local factory produces bottles of spring water. Unfortunately they have experienced some serious problems with their quality control. There are two main problems:

- Every so often the water in a batch is contaminated to such an extent that you cannot see through the bottle.

- There is also a problem with the machine that fixes the lids onto the bottles which causes the bottles to leak when they are turned upside down.

Your task is to design and build a model of a system that could detect these faults and remove the bottles from the conveyor belt.

To complete this project you will need a computer control system such as the **LEGO Dacta Control Lab** or **Robolab**. To build the model you can either use a modelling kit or construct it yourself from resistant materials.

When you have built and tested your system you need to produce a report that explains to the owners of the factory how the system works.

Investigation

The first thing you need to do is find out more about the problem.

- Use the Internet to find out about the ways that factories implement quality control systems.

- Arrange a visit to a local factory to find out about how the company uses automated systems to produce its goods.

- Investigate Design and Technology or Business Studies books that are available in your library or from your teachers.

When you have found some examples of control systems, produce the following:

- A table that lists the input and output devices.

- A flow chart of the whole system.

- A state table of how the system works.

First thoughts

This is a complicated project. You need to break the project down into simple steps. Try writing a simple sentence for each stage of the process. Think about:

- what your model is physically going to look like

- what sensors you are going to use to accurately sense the changes. For example, you could use a light sensor to detect the difference between a normal bottle and a contaminated bottle

- what output devices you might need to remove the unsatisfactory bottles

- what other moving parts might be needed, such as a conveyor belt and a device that can lift and rotate the bottles.

Sketch out some ideas for your model.

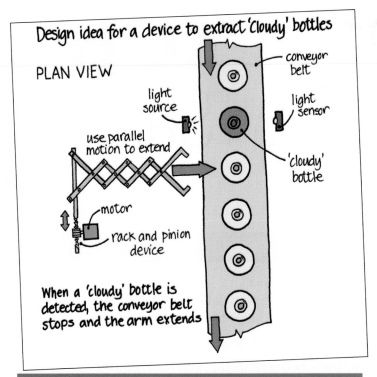

Design idea for a device to extract 'Cloudy' bottles

PLAN VIEW

conveyor belt

light source

light sensor

use parallel motion to extend

'cloudy' bottle

motor

rack and pinion device

When a 'cloudy' bottle is detected, the conveyor belt stops and the arm extends

Planning

By this stage you should have described the process in simple sentences. You should have also formulated some ideas as to what your model will look like. You now need to structure this into a form that will help you write your program.

Draw up a state table (see page 103) that includes all of the steps in the process. Use this to draw a flow chart of the complete process.

Next, you need to build your model and check that all the sensors do in fact provide the required input and that the output devices do the job that they should.

Working at the computer

When you are confident that your flow chart is accurate you need to translate this into the programming language that you are using. The exact detail of this will depend on the actual software that you are using.

If the software is similar to LEGO Dacta **Control Lab** then you will need to break your plan down into procedures and test each separately to ensure that they work.

If your software is based on using symbols to create something that resembles a flow chart then you should have already completed most of the work.

Evaluation

It is important that you plan very carefully how you are going to test your system. It is not sufficient to run the system once and then think that it works. You need to think about all of the different situations that could arise and try to think of ways of simulating them.

For example:

● what happens if a bottle falls over?
● what happens if the bottling plant fails to put any water in the bottle?
● what happens if a bottle cap is faulty and water leaks onto the sensor?

You need to make sure that you have tested all of the separate parts of the system as well.

Draw up a table that lists all of the possible problems that you can think of and include columns for the results of your tests and suggestions for any improvements that you think about while testing the system.

Presentation

When you are writing your presentation remember that the owners of the factory may not be very computer literate, but need to be able to build and maintain the system that you have designed.

You need to describe both the hardware and software. Also it is important to reassure the owners that the system is reliable. You can do this by carefully detailing your testing procedures.

Remember to include as many diagrams as possible, including a screen shot of your final program.

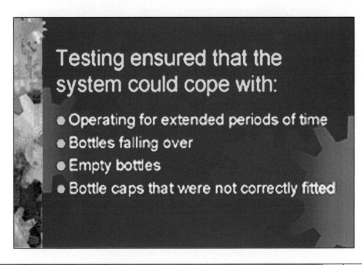

Testing ensured that the system could cope with:

● Operating for extended periods of time
● Bottles falling over
● Empty bottles
● Bottle caps that were not correctly fitted

What's on?

Your local library wants to set up an electronic 'What's on?' in your area. Can you design one for them?

The problem

Your local library wants to provide a computer that young people can use to look up what is happening in their area.

Design and build a database to record 'What's on?' in your area. The database will need to be able:

- to record up to 80 records
- to print out the desired event
- to use existing database software.

Your work should be presented as a working database and a word-processed **Help** manual for the users.

Investigation

Collect your local and national newspapers. Do not forget the 'free' ones!

Find the pages that list:

- concerts
- jumble sales
- collectors' fairs
- sports events
- cinemas and theatres
- car-boot fairs
- youth clubs
- leisure centres.

Look through them carefully and decide which areas you are going to concentrate on. It may help to consider:

- the quantity and quality of information available
- your target audience, e.g. people between the ages of 12 and 29?

Write down a summary giving the reasons why you have chosen particular areas.

First thoughts

Using the newspapers, list the possible fields that you may require for your database. Ask friends and relatives what things they would like to see included.

Draw some mock screens.

- Include the fields that you may require.
- Are there to be different colours for different areas of the screen? For example, all data fields could be yellow and labels could be green.
- Consider graphics – the various sections could be given colourful logos.

Pick out the one that you like the most. Write down the reasons why the chosen one is better than the others.

Working at the computer

Developing your ideas

You now need to ask two main questions about your chosen output screen and the fields it contains.

1) Does the screen contain all the necessary information? For example:
   - The date of the event?
   - Where it is and when it is?
   - Any other special information?
2) Does it look good?
   - Will people want to use it?
   - Is it clear?
   - Is it easy to use?

Making and testing a prototype

Create a simple table and use the **Form Wizard** to make up a test database. Do not worry about what it looks like but make sure that:

- records can be entered easily
- no fields are missing.

Ask a group of people if the information on the screen is what they would expect. Make notes of any improvements that they may suggest.

Creating the working database

Look at your notes and include all the valid suggestions made during testing when designing the **Tables**, **Queries**, **Forms** and **Reports**.

Develop the tables

Use your chosen fields to create a table or tables. Use the full range of validation checks available. This will make sure that when you input the data it is correct. For example, the **Event Date** field could be set so that it is always greater than 'today's date' to prevent the wrong dates being entered.

Develop the screens

Use the tables and Form Wizard to create the output screens. Do not forget to consult your initial sketches and ideas. Remember that you can change any colour fields in **Design View** and use the **colour palette**. Field positions can be changed using **drag and drop** techniques as in any other graphics software.

Develop the queries

Use the tables to create **Queries** of information that are likely to be needed. For example, a query that sorts the database for all events in the next week may be useful. Develop a selection of queries – one for cinema events and one for jumble sales – with a range of date possibilities.

Develop the reports

Use the **Queries** and the **Report Wizard** to create printouts of your database that other students can take away with them. Like the screens, make sure they are clear and easily understood. In **Design View** you can move the fields around using drag and drop, just the same as you did in the screens.

Final testing

Present your database to the same group of people that tried out the prototype.

- What do they think of the screens and printouts?
- Do they think that it is easy to use?
- Have they any suggestions for improvements?

How do I...?

Help manuals are normally books containing instructions or are 'On-Screen' help. You could produce:

- a booklet containing detailed instructions on how to use your database.
- brief 'on-screen' instructions.

Think about using 'screenshots' in your booklet. You may wish to use graphics software for titles and clip art for cartoons to make the booklet interesting to read. Keep the 'on-screen' instructions very simple. You will need to investigate how to add text boxes to your input screens.

Try out the booklet and help screens by asking a friend to follow the instructions that you have written. Get your friend to make some comments and then update your work.

Evaluation

Write an evaluation of the project. You could include the following questions:

- What went well?
- What went wrong?
- If I were to do it again what would I change?
- Did I **Get IT Right**?

Index